Broadway Tails

Heartfelt Stories of Rescued Dogs
Who Became Showbiz Superstars

Bill Berloni

Theatrical Animal Trainer,
and Jim Hanrahan

Foreword by
Bernadette Peters

LYONS PRESS
Guilford, Connecticut
An imprint of Globe Pequot Press

Lyons Press is an imprint of Globe Pequot Press.

Photos courtesy of the author except where otherwise noted.

Photo on page 246 by Michael Carr.

Designed by Diana Nuhn.

The Library of Congress has cataloged the earlier edition as follows:

Berloni, William.
   Broadway tails : heartfelt stories of rescued dogs who became showbiz superstars.
      p. cm.
   ISBN 978-1-59921-353-8
   1. Dogs—New York (State)—New York—Anecdotes. 2. Dogs—Training—New York (State)—New York—Anecdotes. 3. Dogs in the performing arts—New York (State)—New York—Anecdotes. 4. Berloni, William. 5. Animal trainers—New York (State)—New York—Anecdotes. I. Title.
   SF426.2.B45 2008
   792.02′80929—dc22

                                                                                          2008008710

ISBN 978-0-7627-8308-3

Printed in the United States of America

10 9 8 7 6 5 4 3 2 1

I would like to dedicate this book to my wife, Dorothy, who is my present. Without her love, understanding, and support, I couldn't do what I do. I would also like to dedicate this book to my daughter, Jenna, who is my future. If there were no children to pass on the good work to, there would be no hope for a better world.

CONTENTS

Foreword

There is no need to introduce you to the wonderful animal trainer, Bill Berloni, but I will anyway. You know him from training Sandy, the dog in *Annie*—just the beginning of his illustrious career, which has spanned more than three decades. I had the pleasure of working with Bill on a Broadway revival of *Gypsy* in 2003, where he trained a dog and lamb for the show. But that's not the first time we met . . .

Every year in Shubert Alley we hold our annual animal adopt-a-thon, Broadway Barks, which Mary Tyler Moore and I started in 1996. That first year I remember being onstage and looking up and seeing a familiar face among the volunteers. I said to Patty Saccente, who helps produce the event, "Isn't that Bill Berloni, the famous dog trainer, standing up there with the dogs?" Sure enough, he was volunteering with the Humane Society of New York, helping to handle the dogs—and he's been with us every year since! In 2005 we honored him for his great work with Broadway Barks. Bill goes above and beyond with his service to animals, always trying to rescue his animal stars from shelters in order to give them a good life.

In 2010 he joined us for a concert to raise money for Broadway Barks and Broadway Cares/Equity Fights AIDS. He trained the animals and helped to get them adopted that very night. I'm proud to say he received a 2011 Tony Honor, something he so truly deserved.

In this heartwarming collection of stories, Bill takes us behind the scenes, allowing us to experience his wonderful adventures firsthand: training animals for stage and screen (from dogs and cats to birds and rats—and even a pig!); working with Broadway greats; and touring the country with animals in tow. From the very beginning, when he trained his beloved Sandy at the Goodspeed Opera House in Connecticut, to his last Broadway production, *Legally Blonde,* and the upcoming 35th Anniversary production of *Annie,* Bill Berloni is able to capture the magic of these animals onstage. He truly understands them and what they are trying to convey. But most important, he has their safety and best interests at heart. And speaking of heart . . . his is HUGE. Bill Berloni is a godsend to animals and show business!

—Bernadette Peters

Preface

How do you go from a theater apprentice to winning a Tony Honor and being the animal director of a brand new Broadway show? Practice, practice, and lots of dog treats.

It all started when I was two years old, and my mom and dad asked me if I wanted a brother or sister. I said "a dog."

We were living on a small farm in central Connecticut, where my dad, the horticulturist for the city of New Britain, grew flowers and plants for the city parks. It was somewhat secluded and, not having any siblings, the only time I saw other children was at big family events. So mom and dad got me a dog—a big, beautiful male collie named Rexie.

Rexie was my constant companion. Since he was a herding dog, he followed me everywhere and kept me out of trouble. If my mother let me out into the yard and I dared stray toward the woods or the driveway, Rexie would grab me by the seat of my pants and pull me back. I had lots of pets on the farm, so until I went to school, my friends were Rexie, Fritz the cat, and Whitey the bunny.

Now, when I got to kindergarten I was very shy. I wasn't used to being around so many kids, and I didn't know how to interact with them. It wasn't until we did our class play, *Peter Cottontail,* that things started to change. I wouldn't speak or go on stage until our teacher, Mrs. Young, came up with a brilliant idea. She knew that I had a bunny, and she asked if I would bring him in and sit on stage with him. I gladly agreed because I could hold him and talk to him, and he would make me feel calm. So I made my show business debut at the age of four-and-a-half in *Peter Cottontail,* sitting on the edge of the stage in my bunny suit holding Whitey in my lap.

It doesn't sound like much, but I was hooked. From then on, it was living room performances, grade school shows, and high school plays. Although I started college as a business administration major, I soon convinced my parents to let me go into acting. I heard about a famous theater in Connecticut called the Goodspeed Opera House, where they had a summer program for technical apprentices.

And that's where the story began.

Today, thirty-five years later, the story continues. I'm currently working on a revival of *Annie,* the show that started me in this career. And my wife, Dorothy, and I are creating a new show, the first where a dog will be a lead character. It's called *Because of Winn-Dixie,* and it's based on the award-winning book by Kate DiCamillo.

It's not an easy process. It took Dorothy several years to secure the theatrical rights to the novel. But she was persistent and she did it. It was an amazing first step. Today we have a wonderful creative team in place, and we've two Irish wolfhound puppies, Taran and Callie, to play Winn-Dixie.

Of course, we still have a long way to go to meet our goal of opening *Because of Winn-Dixie* on Broadway. And as for the Tony Honor, you will just have to read on to find out about that one. To me there is a more important lesson. The point of developing the show, and the point of all the stories in this book, is to show the wonderful things that rescued animals can do. In the meantime, as long as I have strength to hold a leash, I will keep working, training rescue animals, and hoping for the day there will be no more homeless pets.

Acknowledgments

One of the great gifts the animals have given me over the years is the opportunity to work with some wonderful people. First, are the people who work at shelters and rescue groups. Without their efforts, many of my animal companions wouldn't have survived. And my show business family, the handlers, actors, crews, directors, producers, and support staff who went out of their way to give our animal actors a little love and understanding.

In particular, I want to thank the photographers whose pictures appear in this book: Martha Swope, Joan Marcus, and Paul Kolnick. Not only did they open their files so we could find show photos from decades ago, they are also donating their fees to The Sandy Fund, which supports the work of the Humane Society of New York. I am honored to be in your company.

Readers who would like to donate to The Sandy Fund can send checks to:

The Sandy Fund
c/o The Humane Society of New York
306 East 59th Street
New York, NY 10022

Chapter 1

Somebody Get a Dog

I was having the time of my life. I was nineteen years old and had just completed my first year at Central Connecticut State College as an acting major. In the fall, I would transfer to NYU and begin studying with Stella Adler, the legendary acting teacher. And I was returning to the Goodspeed Opera House for my second year.

Goodspeed is a beautiful Victorian theater built in 1876 on the banks of the Connecticut River. It is dedicated to the American musical and is one of the country's best regional theaters. I had been there the year before as a technical apprentice—which means I had the privilege of working seventy hours a week for no money, but with the opportunity to be around professional actors, designers, directors, and stagehands. I had done community theater, I had done high school theater, I had even done a little college theater my first year, but nothing is the same as being around professionals. Shortly after I returned in the spring of 1976, I was promoted to a paid position, the first time anyone had gone from apprentice to staff member in the same season. I was proud of that.

Pride turned to concern when Michael Price, the executive producer, called me to his office. I had seen Michael around and he had always been friendly, but if I was being called to his office, I assumed I was in big trouble

Andrea McArdle, as Annie, and Sandy in the original Goodspeed Opera House production of *Annie*.
Photo by Wilson Brownell

for something—and I couldn't figure out what. When I got there, he looked me in the eye and said, "How would you like your Equity card?" The Actors' Equity Association is the union that represents professional actors, but there's a catch-22 about joining: You can't be a professional actor in an Equity production unless you have your card—but you can't get your card until you do an Equity show. You have to have someone high up to sponsor you, and now Michael was offering to be my sponsor. Clearly he had recognized my acting ability from a few walk-ons and the way I moved scenery. All I had to do, he said, was find and train a dog for a new show without spending any money. I had never trained a dog before. I didn't know anything about training a performing dog. But in true show-business fashion, I immediately agreed.

I left his office, went outside the building, and started jumping up and down with joy. I ran over to the shop and told everybody that I was going to be an actor. I went to the pay phone and called my mom and dad, I called my best friends, I called everybody I knew, telling them that I finally had my big break. But as I calmed down, I asked myself why I'd been given this important job. The answer was simple—no one else wanted it. The show we were going to do was called *Annie*, based on the classic comic strip, *Little Orphan Annie*. The dog, Sandy, was a major character, and no one thought you could train a dog to play a major character onstage. At the time, however, I was too naive to know that. After all, I had seen dogs play major parts in movies and on TV, so I didn't see why it couldn't be done for this show. What I didn't understand at that point was that what we see on screen is often the result of days of work, with multiple takes. Onstage, there would only be one chance to get it right—every night and in front of a live audience. It had never been done before.

Then there was the problem of the budget—or lack of one. No one would lend us a pet for the production, and buying a dog was out of the question. One of the crew suggested the best bet was to try the local dog pounds. So on Monday, my day off, I took the props department's Polaroid camera and beat-up green travel van and I went dog shopping.

If you remember the comic strip, Sandy didn't look like a real dog. He was a big red mutt with blank eyes, pointy ears, a white muzzle, and a big fluffy tail. The creators of the show knew we'd never find a real dog that looked like that, so I was told to get a medium-sized dog of sandy color and no distinguishable breed. Back in 1976, there weren't many animal shelters like the ones we know today, staffed by wonderful volunteers. In Connecticut at that time, most towns had dog pounds—generally a few pens or cages behind the town garage—where the local animal control officers kept strays. I went from town to town, walking out to look at two or three dogs at a time: skinny, shivering, huddling in the corner, or attacking the bars. I had never seen animals in conditions like these before. Sometimes I would show up and there would be nobody there, and I'd find the dogs with no food or water. As the day progressed and I didn't find any dogs that met our description, I became more and more disheartened. I made myself a promise—if I ever got a dog, I would rescue it from a shelter.

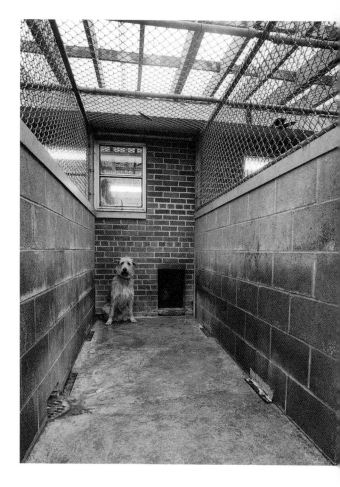

Late in the afternoon, I ended up at the Connecticut Humane Society, which was a shelter rather than a pound. If you found a stray or couldn't keep a pet, you could bring it there voluntarily. It looked like a jail—an old brick building with two long extensions that had twenty-five cement-and-chain-link runs on each side of a long hallway. Most of the pounds had no more than three or four dogs. The Connecticut Humane Society had a hundred. As I started walking past the cages, most dogs were jumping and

barking, while some just cowered in the corner. The sound was deafening and the smell, overwhelming. I didn't see any dogs that matched our description, and I was getting more and more depressed. I almost left after going through the first wing, but something said, go down the other side.

The first time I saw him, he was sitting in the shadows, not barking or jumping. As I looked closer, I could see he was medium-sized, of no particular breed, and although his coat was wet and dirty, it was definitely a sandy color. When I stopped and knelt down, he slowly turned his head over his shoulder and looked at me with the biggest, saddest brown eyes I had ever seen. The card on the front of the cage said simply: 1½ YEARS OLD, MALE, STRAY, NO NAME. I got the attention of the attendant, and I asked him if I could bring the dog out. Over the racket, he yelled: "He's been pretty badly abused. He doesn't like people. I've got to get a rope to get him out."

He walked away, but I couldn't wait. I knelt again and opened the cage. I stuck out my hand and called, "It's okay, boy. Come here . . . come here." He looked at me with those sad eyes for what seemed like the longest time. Then he crept over to me, lay down on the floor, and let me pet him. I smiled and told him everything was going to be okay. I'm not sure when I realized the attendant was standing behind me, his mouth hanging open. The dog looked at him and ran to the back of the cage.

"He's never done that with any of us. I can't believe that he would come up to you. Do you still want me to take him out?"

I said no. The dog had come to me and wouldn't come to anyone else. That was all I needed to know. At the front desk, I explained the situation to a disbelieving staff and told them I would be back to pick up the dog as soon as I got approval from the director or producer. They laughed at me. One of the staff said, "Sorry, you've got to take him today or we're going to put him down tomorrow." That was probably the worst moment of a terrible day. I couldn't believe what I was hearing. It had never occurred to me that the Humane Society would kill dogs. I was sure it was a mistake. They must have misunderstood me. They didn't have to put him down, I told them. I would be back for him if they could only wait. I pleaded with them to give me a little more time.

"We keep them for seven days and that's it."

I had been upset before; now I was getting frantic. I wanted to save this dog. Something was telling me I *had* to save this dog. "How much does he cost?" I asked.

"Seven dollars."

I pulled out all the money I had on me: three dollars. I asked them to take it as a deposit. I begged them to lend me four dollars, promising I would be back in the morning. Nothing I said made any difference. Maybe working in that place had hardened them. Maybe they had heard too many people promise to come back and then not show up. Maybe they thought I was crazy. But they weren't about to bend the rules, even if it meant the dog had to die.

I was miserable. They were closing in fifteen minutes; there was no way I could get the money and get back in time. I felt like I was condemning the dog to death. I asked if I could go say good-bye. He was still cowering in his cage, but he turned to look at me. All I could say through my tears was,

"Don't worry, it'll be okay," hoping that however they put him to sleep, it would be painless and merciful.

Driving back to the Goodspeed, I decided there was one more chance to save him. If I could get someone to give the approval, we could call the Humane Society that night and get a stay of execution—but when I got to the theater, there was no one around who could give me permission to get the dog.

My roommate that summer was a guy by the name of John Camp, a fun, upbeat guy who was training a golden retriever puppy. That night as we were lying in our room, John said to me, "What are you so upset about? Just go back in the morning before they open the doors and adopt this dog."

"But nobody's approved him."

"So what? If they don't like him, get him a home, give him away. What's the big deal?"

I borrowed four dollars from the other apprentices and crew. The next morning I called up my best friend from high school, Dave Capodeice, and we drove to the Humane Society. We got there at 6:30 A.M. and waited by the back door. The staff was surprised to see us when they arrived half an hour later. We led the dog to the truck and loaded him in. Even though he immediately cowered in the back, I was happy. Dave had his doubts. "This dog isn't going to work, Bill. He's terrified, he looks awful, and he's probably starving."

I said, "Well, then, the first thing we should do is get him something to eat." We stopped at a McDonald's and I used the last few coins I had in my pocket to buy him a hamburger. When I unwrapped it and tried to offer it to him, he avoided me. Finally, I put the hamburger down and went to the front seat. While Dave and I watched, the dog looked at us, looked at the hamburger, crept up to it, and ate it in one gulp. I said, "Good boy—there you go." He looked at me and then ran back to his hiding place. Things didn't get any better when we returned to the Opera House. As the crew members gathered around, the dog kept hiding behind my legs. He wouldn't let anybody touch him. Everyone thought I had made a big mistake.

My girlfriend, Jude, who also worked in the props department, said, "He needs a bath, maybe that'll help." I agreed, so we got some dish soap and brought him up to the paint sink on the second floor of the scenic shop. He struggled and fought, but as the dirt was washed away, I could see a beautiful sandy coat.

"What are you going to call him?"

Up until that point, I hadn't thought about a name. It dawned on me that it would probably make sense to call him by his character name so he wouldn't be confused. I said, "How about Sandy?"

Toweling Sandy dry made us realize how thin he actually was. I took some money out of the prop fund and we went to buy dog food and a bowl. By now, even though he was terrified of everything and everyone, he was starting to stick by me. By the end of that first day he had met twenty or thirty people, had a bath, gone to the Feed & Green store, and come back to the scenic shop. I tied him up in the back of the prop shop, where it was nice and quiet, with a bowl of water and a blanket so that I could get to work building scenery. I would go and visit him whenever I could. He spent the day watching every move I made in the shop.

The next morning I tied him up to the same place where he could see me while I worked. He was a little less frightened, and the crew was great about going slow around him and trying to make friends. About the middle of the afternoon, I took Sandy over to the theater and tied him to the front of the stage while we did some repair work. I turned around to check on him, and there was Martin Charnin—who had conceived the show, written the lyrics, and was directing—gently petting him. I started to blurt out, "Mr. Charnin, this is . . ."

Martin looked at me and said, "He's perfect. This is our Sandy." Without even asking, I had the director's okay.

The next task was training Sandy to be in the show. In his big scene, all he had to do was come onstage to Annie, lie down while she was questioned by a policeman, then come when Annie called his name. Pretty simple stuff—until you remember that he had to do it onstage in front of hundreds of people.

There were no books about training an animal for the stage that I could read. All I had to go on was my own experience. I remembered growing up with my collie, Rexie. He did a lot of things without any training. Some of it was instinct—he was a herding dog, so when I was little, he naturally followed me around and made sure I stayed in the yard. Some of it was being part of our family—he loved us, he trusted us, he learned from our daily routine. He knew when I got home from school and would meet me at the bus. And he knew that the sound of the can opener meant dinner.

So, to me, it seemed like those were the two keys to training a dog. The first part would be easier—building on what Sandy did naturally. The second part, particularly with a dog like Sandy who had been abused, was more difficult. He had to learn to trust us, particularly me. He had to learn that he was safe with us, particularly when he was onstage. He had to know that we wouldn't let him be hurt again. If I could make Sandy think that the theater was his home and we were his family, maybe he could learn to follow our routine, just like Rexie had. That's what I set out to do.

Sandy became my shadow—wherever I went, he went. Anyone I met, he met, too. He came to the shop every day, and little by little he got used to the loud noises and banging. Little by little, he got used to all the people in the crew. Every night I would bring him over to the theater and keep him in the green room, where all the actors hang out and take their breaks. He became a regular. During scene changes and intermission, I would bring him up onstage and he would lie there, or he'd stay next to me in the wings, watching the work.

Things were going really well. Over the next few weeks, I made my debut as a professional actor in a small role in the second show of the season. Sandy was making great progress. And we began work on *Annie*—we were building the sets, and the cast came up to East Haddam to begin rehearsals.

Annie was being played by a young actress named Kristen Vigard, who was living in the actors' house, next door to the tech house where I lived. I changed my routine so that each morning and each evening I would walk Sandy over to Kristen's room, where she would feed him and pet him. During rehearsals we would get time together to go over our big scene. It would start when I'd say, "Go see Kristen," and she'd give him a treat. I'd have Sandy lie down while Kristen and I read the lines of dialogue. On cue, he was supposed to run over, jump up, and put his paws on Kristen's shoulders. As Sandy became more outgoing, he would jump up on people as he greeted them, so all we had to do was encourage this. Little by little I saw a real connection growing between Kristen and Sandy, and I saw him fall into the pattern we wanted. Now all we had to do was make sure he got used to the audience and wasn't frightened by them.

What I didn't realize at the time was that I had already done that. By bringing Sandy to the shop every day and to the theater every night, he'd already become completely comfortable with the noise and action of a live performance.

Two weeks before *Annie* opened, the shop was buzzing as the scenery was being assembled. While I was working in the back, Sandy got in a bit of trouble when he managed to walk across a freshly painted backdrop. The scenic artist got very upset and insisted that Jude get Sandy out of the way. Since the shop was getting more and more hectic, she knew that was the best thing to do. She took Sandy and tied him out under a shade tree with a bowl of water.

It was a hot, sticky July day. Instead of staying under the tree, Sandy tried to find a place where it was even cooler, in the dirt under one of our trucks. No one knew he was there until my roommate, John Camp, tried to take the truck to make a delivery. As he pulled away, he heard a dog scream. He had run Sandy over. Within seconds, I was running out of the shop. Sandy dragged himself toward me with his front paws, unable to stand, screaming in pain. I picked him up, carried him into the truck, and rushed him to the vet. The doctor saw him immediately, sedated him because he was in so much pain, and said we wouldn't know anything until he took some X-rays.

About forty-five minutes later, the vet showed us the X-rays. We had gotten lucky. Because the dirt in the parking lot was so soft, it had given way under Sandy as the truck rolled over him. As a result, nothing was broken, although one rear leg had been dislocated. The vet had put it back into place and said there should be no permanent damage. But, he told us, Sandy was going to need to be on cage rest for two weeks before the bandages could come off.

We were twelve days away from opening night.

The vet said it was unlikely he'd be able to walk by then. Before I left, I visited Sandy in the recovery area. He was still groggy from the anesthesia. I opened the cage door and gently petted his head. He opened his eyes and tried to stick his tongue out to lick me. I sat there petting him and crying. I was glad he was alive and would get better, but I didn't know how to break the news to the cast and crew that we had lost our dog. When I got back to the theater, I reported to Michael Price and Martin Charnin. They were extremely upset. I was told to find another dog—quick. Adding to the pressure, Michael said he was holding Jude and John responsible and would fire them if we didn't have a dog for the show.

The next day the vet allowed Sandy to come home. We made a soft bed for him in the tech house and another in the shop, so he could lie down and watch us. Four or five times a day I would pick him up and carry him outside so that he could relieve himself, then bring him back to his pillow.

I began the depressing process of revisiting all the local pounds, but there were no sandy-colored dogs available. Meanwhile, Sandy was getting restless. Four days after the accident, we were having a hard time keeping him on the bed. It seemed obvious to me that he missed his routine and he missed being with his family. Finally, six days after the accident, I decided Sandy knew best—if he felt well enough to walk, I would let him walk. He was able to limp around on three legs and made it clear he was ready to run and play, even while I was trying to keep him calm. That's how Martin Charnin found us one day. He couldn't believe Sandy was walking. I pointed out that he was still bandaged.

"That's okay, that's okay," he said. "We can leave the bandage on. We can even write it into the script! The audience will really feel sorry for him." Which they did.

A week after the accident, the vet examined Sandy again. He called his recovery a miracle. "The only way he could get better this fast is because he really *wants* to get better," he told me. "And he wants to get better because of you. This dog really loves you." He gave me a new Ace bandage and told me to take it off at night when Sandy was sleeping, but to keep it on during the day when he was walking.

So Sandy went back into rehearsal, limping, but incredibly happy to get back to Kristen and the crew, who were more than happy to make a fuss over him. Every day he got a little stronger, even as things got crazier with opening night approaching. He was perfect during rehearsals, even trying to jump up on Kristen, though we tried to stop him.

At a summer stock theater like Goodspeed, the most hectic time is the changeover between two shows. You give the final performance of one show on Sunday night, and then the crew works most of the night to take down the old set and build the new one. Monday afternoon, there's a tech rehearsal, where the actors come onstage and we move the scenery cue by cue, focusing the lights and making adjustments. Dress rehearsal is

Sandy rehearsing
his big scene.
Photo by Michael Carr

Monday night. On Tuesday afternoon you have your last rehearsal, and the new show opens that night.

The changeover for *Annie* did not go well. We had trouble getting the set into the theater and trouble getting it to work. We worked on it all day Monday with hardly a break. The tech rehearsal didn't start until Monday night—and even after five hours, the complicated set changes still weren't working right. In fact, we didn't even finish because it was past midnight and we had to get the kids to bed. After working for thirty-six straight hours, they let us get some sleep, but we had to be back at 8:00 A.M. on Tuesday to prepare for dress rehearsal.

We worked all that morning on the set. The dress rehearsal didn't start until Tuesday afternoon, just hours before the show opened. Between the kids not knowing their lines and the set not working, it was one of the worst dress rehearsals we had ever had. But Sandy went out there in his Ace bandage and did his scene. Then, as we took our dinner break, we heard there were severe storm warnings for the area.

The theater was probably half full for the first performance of *Annie*. As the overture started, I took the Ace bandage off of Sandy's leg so the audience wouldn't see it. When it was time for his scene, Sandy saw Kristen onstage and went to her just like he had in all of the rehearsals. The audience let out a collective, "Awww." This was new, so Sandy stopped to take a look at the people. Then he went over and lay down next to Kristen while she sang her big song, "Tomorrow." When his cue came, he trotted over to Kristen, and before she could grab his leash, he jumped up and put his paws on her shoulders. I was astounded. He had remembered what we wanted him to do. He did it for us even though he was hurting. He looked over at me offstage as if to say, "It's okay, Bill."

Unfortunately, the rest of the show did not go as well. A hurricane hit at intermission, and half the audience left. We lost power and had to start the second act using a generator, which lit up only a few lights. The show was going slowly—the curtain didn't come down till 11:30. We hadn't even finished building the supports for sets for the last scene, so the stagehands had to hold up the walls. But I was smiling. Sandy had come through for me. The dog no one wanted. The dog that was hours away from being put to sleep. The dog that everybody thought couldn't do it. The dog that had been run over by a truck just twelve days earlier. He had done everything we had asked him to do.

The first night of any new show is always a disaster—that's what summer stock is about. The show was changing every day—we finished the sets, the script was rewritten, new numbers were added, and old ones taken out. Then, two weeks into the run, the creators made a major decision. They decided, in order to get the audience really rooting for Annie, they needed a different kind of performance. They needed a kid who was tougher, with street smarts, someone optimistic enough to survive the Great Depression. While Kristen Vigard was a very bright, talented actress, they didn't think she could give that kind of performance. So they replaced Kristen with Andrea McArdle, who had been playing one of the orphans.

After the Sunday-night performance, Martin Charnin took Kristen aside and told her what was happening. She was upset, but like a true professional, she understood it was for the good of the show. Then Martin went to Andrea. With Sandy by their side, he asked her if she would like to take over the role. She said, "Sure." They started rehearsing that night. We worked all day Monday and all day Tuesday. I was worried because I had spent almost six weeks getting this dog to think that Kristen was the little girl he should love, and now a brand-new kid was coming along. But

Andrea had a dog at home and she knew what to do. She hugged Sandy and kissed him and played with him, and in twenty-four hours, not only did she take us all by storm, but she had Sandy falling in love with her, too. By Tuesday night, instead of going out for a treat from Kristen, Sandy was going out to play with Andrea, which was a totally different feeling. At that point things really began to change. The audience started cheering for Annie instead of acting like they were watching a comic strip. We started to feel that maybe this musical had a chance.

As the season drew to a close, I began to worry about what I would do with Sandy. I was going to be sharing a New York City apartment with two other people from the Opera House. I didn't see any way that I could afford to take Sandy with me. I thought that my parents would take him, but they already had a dog at home and didn't want another. I was shocked because I never thought my parents would turn him down. I thought I'd be able to see him every time I came home.

A week before the show was scheduled to close, the creators told Michael Price they wanted to extend the run. They thought the musical was going in the right direction. Michael said he couldn't afford it—reviews had been poor, the box office was bad, and the show was over budget. The only way it could continue was if the creators paid everyone's salary. The creators agreed to pay for a two-week extension. This was another problem for me—I couldn't stay past September 1. I had classes at NYU, and I didn't want to miss my first day at Stella Adler's studio. Patrick O'Leary, one of my friends who would be sharing the apartment, offered to stay, take care of Sandy, and continue trying to find him a home.

It was very hard, but I slowly started to pull myself away from Sandy. But every time Patrick would lead him away, he would look back at me over his shoulder with those sad, sad eyes. At the same time, we were putting up adoption posters and asking friends and family if they would take him, but we couldn't find him a home.

Then I was contacted by one of Goodspeed's board members, a wonderful lady named Norma Terris. She had been a famous Broadway actress, appearing in the original production of *Showboat*, along with many other shows. Now she was in her seventies, lived locally, and spent her time promoting animal welfare. She had followed the story of Sandy, and when she heard that I was looking for a home for him, she invited me over for lunch at her mansion on the banks of the Connecticut River. All during my visit, she kept saying that Sandy belonged with me and I couldn't give him up. No matter what excuse I made, she stuck to her point: "If you really love someone, you'll find a way to make it work."

As I said good-bye to Sandy, I cried very hard. He didn't understand why I was upset. As I drove away, I could see him in the rearview mirror, straining against the leash as he tried to follow me.

The night I moved into my fifth-floor walk-up, I called Patrick to see how things were going. He had bad news. Sandy wasn't eating. He was lethargic. He barely went out onstage, and he was no longer jumping up on Andrea. No one had come forward to adopt him. As the week progressed, things just got worse. On that Friday I got a call from Norma Terris.

"Young man," she said, obviously concerned, "this dog is very upset that you're not there. You must take care of this dog."

"But Miss Terris, I can't afford . . ."

That's when she made the best offer anyone has ever made to me. She said, "Young man, I will make a promise to you if you will make a promise to me. I will fund the cost of having the dog with you, if you promise to take care of him for the rest of his life." At first I tried to refuse, because I didn't want to take money from a stranger—but she insisted. So, on Saturday, I drove back to Connecticut to do the final shows. Sandy was thrilled— he jumped all over me, knocked me down, and licked my face. On Sunday evening, after the final curtain, Patrick, Sandy, and I got in the car and drove to New York City. I looked down at Sandy lying across the backseat with his head on my lap and thought, Well, if I'm going to be a starving actor, I might as well have a dog that's going to starve with me.

Chapter 2

On Broadway

In September 1976 I had moved to Greenwich Village in New York and was living my dream: I was a starving actor. I had my Equity card. I was attending NYU and studying with acting legend Stella Adler. I had my dog. Life couldn't have gotten much better.

Then in November I got a call from the office of the famous director Mike Nichols. Mike was making his producing debut with the Broadway production of *Annie*—would I be interested in working on the show? It would have an out-of-town tryout in Washington, D.C., in January 1977, and then open on Broadway in April. It took a while before the shock wore off, and when it did, I realized the only way for me to work with Mike Nichols was to drop out of school and pretend to be an animal trainer. The last time I pretended, I got my Equity card and a great dog out of it. This could be my lucky break.

A few days later I was in the office of Peter Neufeld and Tyler Gatchell, the general managers for the show. At first, I think they were just as surprised to see this kid walk in as I was to be in a real New York theater office. As we talked, they must have sensed the sheer terror I was feeling. Peter finally came right out and asked, "Can you train this dog?" I told them I had made the whole process up at Goodspeed and had no idea if I could do

In seven years on Broadway, Sandy starred with five different Annies: Andrea McArdle (left), and from top to bottom, Shelley Bruce, Sarah Jessica Parker, Allison Smith, and Alyson Kirk.

Photo by Martha Swope, © New York Public Library for the Performing Arts

Everyone likes getting their hair done.
Photo by Michael Carr

it again. They said they couldn't hire a novice for such an important part of the show and asked if I would work with a "real" trainer. "Gladly," I said. Then they asked how much I wanted. *How much?*, I thought. *They were going to pay me?* It must have shown on my face, because they realized they had a sucker. They offered me $300 a week plus my hotel in Washington, D.C. Wow! I thought I'd hit the jackpot. Little did I know, the actor's minimum was $600 a week for chorus, and I was working with a star. But I gladly took it. Even if I did the show for ten weeks, I could finance college for a year!

The "real" trainer they hired had handled dogs in the military—he was big, bad, and bald. His training method was all about intimidation. He showed me how to use a metal choke collar on a dog—I remember him dragging Sandy away from me and turning quickly and jerking the collar, which flipped Sandy over. I was horrified. I didn't have the heart to hurt Sandy like he did. Sandy started to shake but didn't leave his side. In that moment I felt I had made a horrible decision. If this was what animal training was about, I wanted out.

I never went back to finish the class but learned a lot about how I wouldn't train a dog. I went back to the general managers and said I wanted to quit because the training was so aggressive. They said they didn't care how I handled the training, just get it done or they'd sue for breach of contract. I remember calling my mentor, Norma Terris. When I told her about the trainer, she scoffed. "Young man, you don't need anyone to tell you what to do. You and Sandy have something special. Trust him, and yourself, and it will be fine." That was the best advice I ever took from a human about animal training.

The crazy thing is, if you look at the original credits for *Annie*, this guy is listed as the trainer, even though he never set foot in the theater. I was only listed as Sandy's owner. That was before we became a hit and they changed the credits.

The general managers reminded me I needed an understudy in case Sandy got sick. Holy cow; two dogs to train. I had promised myself that if I ever got another dog, I would rescue one. I went up to the American Society for the Prevention of Cruelty to Animals in Manhattan. The first dog I found was a calm, six-month-old puppy that had brown, scruffy fur. He was very cute. He had been a stray, was thin, and they said he had a cold. He slowly walked out of his cage and let me pet him and pick him up. I thought this little guy was sweet and had a personality that would be easy to train, so I adopted him. I thought maybe my luck was changing.

But the puppy's cold got worse. Two days later I took him to the vet and found he didn't have a cold, he had distemper. It was so advanced, the vet recommended euthanasia. I couldn't believe my ears. It was incurable and he was going down fast, so I had to agree. It was the first time I ever had to make that decision. After it was over, the vet asked if the puppy had come in contact with any other dogs. He had just spent two days with Sandy in my apartment. Fortunately, Sandy had been vaccinated for distemper but we had to wait ten days to make sure he was clear. I was a wreck worrying about him the whole time.

Rehearsals were getting close. I had Sandy doing his old tricks, but I had no understudy. After visiting shelters all around New York City, I found a healthy red collie mix with pointy ears that looked like the dog in the comic strip. I adopted him and called him Arf.

When rehearsals began, I was mesmerized. They had brought in famed choreographer Peter Gennaro, added a few more chorus people, and

Dorothy Loudon was now playing Miss Hannigan. When Sandy saw Andrea McArdle, he went crazy. He loved her so much. In fact, as happy as Sandy was with me, he seemed even happier to be back in a rehearsal room. As I sat down in the semicircle surrounding the piano and heard the show read and sung, I felt I was a part of theater history being made. Imagine my surprise when I heard Sandy's part had gone from two scenes to four! A scene had been written where he barks to protect Annie before he gets lost. Then halfway through the first act, after a number called "NYC," Martin Charnin read, "Sandy enters slowly from stage right, sits center stage, looks right, looks left, and exits stage left."

I almost fell off my chair. Because we had gone against conventional wisdom and successfully put a dog in the show, the creators thought we could do more. Getting Sandy to bark wouldn't be hard. At Goodspeed, he had shown an immediate dislike for one of the actors when he wore a policeman's uniform. We could use that by having the actor threaten to take Annie back to the orphanage. Sandy would bark to protect her. The real problem was the big "NYC" cue, which sounded so simple when Martin read it. I couldn't think of a way to get Sandy to stop at center stage. If I put him in one wing and called him from the other, he was going to come running right to me. Then, one day, I inadvertently dropped a treat on the floor. Sandy came running, skidded to a stop, ate it, then continued to me. Aha!

I asked Martin if I could get someone to drop a treat onstage as they were exiting, and he said sure. When we used hard treats, they bounced. As a poor, starving actor, I was eating lots of bologna sandwiches for lunch, so we tried that, and Sandy went right for it. When he reached the treat, I would whisper, "Sit." Someone would make a sound stage right, he would look that way, then I would make a sound stage left, and he would look that way. Finally, I would call him off. It became affectionately known as the "Baloney drop," which was a play on my last name. That small piece of processed meat created one of the most moving moments in Broadway history.

We went to Washington, D.C., not knowing what to expect. The cast was excused from dress rehearsal so we could go to the White House and perform for President Carter and all fifty governors. I remember walking up the driveway to the East Room, feeling a sense of pride that I was going to meet and entertain the president of the United States. Then I was jerked back to reality when Sandy pulled on his lead to leave his mark on a tree by the White House lawn.

The rest of that spring was a blur. *Annie* was a huge hit and broke all box office records at the Kennedy Center. We came to New York on a cloud. The reviews acknowledged Sandy's performance, and I became a famous animal trainer at the age of twenty. The other trainer was never mentioned again, and soon the credits were changed. It was all strange and exciting, but Sandy and the kids kept me grounded.

Andrea and Sandy, of course, became a legendary Broadway couple. For the next year she and Sandy would do eight shows a week, multiple television appearances, award shows, charity events, and countless other public appearances—and because they loved each other, it all seemed effortless.

When he was tired, she helped him out; and when she was sad, he'd come over and give her a kiss. (Sandy never kissed anyone except Andrea and me.) Through it all, though, they remained a kid and her dog, and I did my best to keep it that way. Andrea loved practical jokes and was constantly pulling pranks—like the time she made a smiley face with cotton balls and stuck it on the back of "Daddy Warbuck's" black tuxedo during curtain call. Or the time she brought in a new toy called Slime and shook everyone's hand onstage with it.

Sandy had his moments, too. Our original conductor, Peter Howard, opened the show using his favorite old wooden baton. About six months into the show, it broke, and the cast replaced it with a brand-new white one. That night, as Andrea sang the hit song, "Tomorrow," Sandy noticed something different in the pit. He sat up and started watching this white stick. As it went up, his head went up—as it went down, his head went down. The audience very quickly caught on that he was watching the conductor and started to laugh. And when this white thing didn't stop, Sandy started doing little "woofs" at it, which happened to fall on the beat of the music. Andrea handled it like a pro, and "Tomorrow" never received as much applause as it did on the night that Sandy sang along.

For our first year, all the stars got applause when they first entered. One night it was raining heavily, and we held the curtain because the sold-out audience had had such a hard time getting there. As a result, they weren't in the best mood. When Sandy made his first entrance, he got halfway to Andrea and stopped dead. He knew something was different but couldn't figure out what it was. I could see him think, *Where is all that noise those people make?* So he slowly turned his head and looked out into the theater. The audience soon realized Sandy was checking them out and ignoring Andrea, who was saying *Come here, boy,* over and over. They began to laugh. He stared. They laughed harder. He still stared. They were roaring now. He still stared. They finally applauded, and he went on with the show.

Of all the celebrities who came to the show, Sandy's favorite was Benji. Our press agent heard Benji was coming to New York for the opening of his new film and arranged a photo op. His owner and trainer, Frank Inn, was one of the best in Hollywood, and I was a little nervous about meeting him. Sandy did a few behaviors in the show and not much else. I felt that was enough. When Frank and Benji arrived, Sandy went crazy; it wasn't until Frank said, "Come here, girl," that I understood why. Sandy was in love, and it took all my strength to hold him back. All Sandy wanted to do was have a love scene with Benji, and I had to put Andrea in the middle with her arms locked around Sandy's neck to get the picture—which made the front page of the *Daily News* the next day.

Frank did a demonstration for us. Benji knew twenty or thirty behaviors, which she did effortlessly. As my self-esteem was running out, I realized that when Frank was not interacting with Benji, she did not move. Andrea had noticed it too. Benji looked like she was programmed to never take her eyes off of Frank. The more we watched, the sadder we became. After Frank and Benji got in their limo and went off, Andrea hugged Sandy and said she felt so sorry for Benji. "It's like she has no free will. Sandy may not be as trained as Benji, but at least he's happy."

After we had been running for about a year, Sandy's understudy Arf died suddenly. I returned from having just walked the two dogs when he began screaming. He convulsed violently and died in my arms in the hallway outside my dressing room. It was very traumatic because the whole backstage area could hear his screams. Andrea and the kids were so upset, we had to hold the curtain for a half-hour to calm them all down. At first we thought it was poison from some deranged fan, but an autopsy showed that a brain tumor had burst in his head. We missed that dog a lot because he was very sweet, and we were sad that he never got a chance to go on.

A few weeks earlier, I had adopted a stray dog that had been found on Park Avenue. He had been badly abused—someone had poured a flammable substance on his hindquarters and set him on fire. The poor creature was so frightened that he tried to bite any human who came near him. Since this dog looked like a Sandy dog, the woman who found him called me. I knew he would probably be euthanized because no one would want to pay

"And my friend will have the steak . . . raw."

Photo by Michael Carr

his medical expenses, so I said I would take him. I called him O'Malley after my Irish roommate, Patrick.

I brought O'Malley to my vet and the prognosis was bad. He had scar tissue on the base of his tail and legs where he had been burned. He had all sorts of intestinal worms. But the worst news was that he had heartworms. The medicine used to treat heartworms is based on arsenic—so if the worms don't kill the dog, the treatment might. My vet successfully administered the cure but said O'Malley would need a stress-free environment for at least a month, to let his heart recover. Fortunately, I had an unfinished basement in the house I had just bought, so I made him a little apartment down there. When I first turned him loose, all he did was hide. I couldn't get close enough to put a leash on him without him lunging and trying to bite me.

Finally, after six weeks of him still trying to attack me, I thought it was time this dog learned I wasn't a bad person. I got an old overcoat and some car-washing gloves and went downstairs. In a very calm voice, I kept saying *Good boy*. I tried to pet him. As soon as I got close to him, he bit me on the sleeve of the coat and held on. I didn't run, I just let him bite. He kept at it for an hour and a half. But when he was so tired he couldn't move, he saw that all I wanted to do was pet him, so he finally let me. And slowly but surely, after that night I could pet him, touch him, take him out, and have others touch him. I knew if he really got scared he was ready to defend himself, but I made sure he was never placed in that kind of situation. I didn't think I'd ever be able to use him in the show because he had been so abused. But it was like a miracle. Once he learned to trust me and to believe that I truly cared for him, he was one of the best-trained dogs I had. He was so willing to please. I always believe that animals know when you save their lives and are appreciative.

Anyway, when Arf died, I was left without an understudy. O'Malley was healthy by that time, and he trusted me, but he was still totally untrained. To fulfill my contract, I decided to bring O'Malley in. Our cast was so kind, loving, and understanding, that very soon he learned to trust many people. Within six months, except for the black scars on his hindquarters (which we covered with makeup because the hair never grew back), you'd have thought he was the happiest dog in the world. And Sandy must have known O'Malley needed some extra help, because he never had a problem with him and accepted him as part of our family.

While the show was running, I rehearsed with Andrea's understudy, Shelley Bruce, who took over the role when Andrea left. Shelley lived in New Jersey and had grown up with dogs. She had also been with us since the Goodspeed production and was friendly with Sandy. Every Thursday we'd run the show in understudy rehearsal, and Sandy would do his behaviors. When Shelley went on for Andrea, Sandy was a little concerned, but still did fine. Everything went smoothly.

The time finally came when Andrea had to move on. It was a very sad time for us all. You become like a family, and now one of the kids was all grown up and leaving. We all knew we would see Andrea again, but Sandy was somewhat concerned her last night, when everyone was crying. I'm sure he figured, *Those crazy humans are acting up again*, and went on.

The following Tuesday, Shelley came in, and while Sandy did the show, I could see him looking around for Andrea. As the week progressed, he became more and more lethargic; he was missing his first love. Try as we might to play with him, kiss him, and talk to him, he just moped around. Then I remembered the old saying, "The way to a man's heart is through his stomach." I had always given Sandy Milk-Bones as rewards in the show, but now I decided I had to up the ante. The theater was next door to the world-famous Gallagher's Restaurant, where we had most of our parties. Sandy ate there so often, his picture is still on the wall today. We told them the problem and they started sending over their best prime rib. The first time Shelley gave him some, he was a little surprised—but after that, he followed her around like a little lost puppy. We were soon able to eliminate the prime rib because Sandy came to love Shelley for herself.

One of our more comical moments came with Sarah Jessica Parker, our third Annie. She was one of eight children of Barbara and Paul Forste. Her parents and all the kids were in show business at one time or another. They would often do tours, performing in *The Sound of Music* or *Peter Pan* as a family. I was not much older than Sarah's oldest brother, so they just adopted me like another kid. Sarah had been brought in to understudy Shelley when Andrea left. She was the first kid I worked with who didn't have much experience with dogs. Her family traveled a lot, so they had never had a dog—they were really cat people. But because of our friendship and her professionalism, Sarah worked hard learning how to relate to Sandy. Of course, Sandy went through another depression when Shelley left, but a little prime rib solved that problem.

While Sarah was playing the role, we were asked to appear on a Bob Hope special being filmed in New York. Sandy had done many television spots, but this one was a little different—Sarah would be singing live with Sandy in front of twenty thousand troops on the deck of the USS *Iwo Jima*. Nothing about the performance would faze Sandy, but I knew he had never been near anything like the unusual sounds and smells of a battleship. The day came, and we were picked up by limo and taken to the ship, which was docked in New York harbor. Because Sarah and Sandy were such pros, they had no rehearsal planned, just two takes—one to check the sound level with the orchestra, and an extra one for good luck.

When it came time to perform, we were taken to the deck. It was an incredible sight—thousands of servicemen and -women were packed in, all over the ship. There was a big stage with a full orchestra behind us. They put a body mike on Sarah so she wouldn't have to hold a mike, and when Sarah and Sandy made their entrance and she sang our hit song, "Tomorrow," the troops went wild. When she was done with the first take, I went up and rewarded Sandy and praised Sarah and stayed with them for a few moments. Unfortunately, it was a hot July day, and the sun was beating down on the deck. Sandy was quite warm and was panting to cool himself off. Now, in private, Sarah would kid me about the dogs, but in public, she would hug and kiss Sandy. In that minute, while we were waiting for them to set up the next take, Sandy accidentally salivated on her arm. With a big smile on her face, Sarah leaned over and in a voice of sheer disgust whispered in my ear, "Gross! He drooled on me." As she said the last word, we heard her voice echo from the back of the ship and realized her mike was still on. Twenty thousand troops began to laugh and applaud. The look on Sarah's face was utter embarrassment, but I fell over laughing. From then on Sarah would wait until we were completely alone to joke about Sandy. Sarah ultimately grew up to be a true dog lover.

When Sarah outgrew the role, she was replaced by Allison Smith. Allison was our youngest Annie—she was ten years old and had no theater experience except for a small role in *Evita*. Allison was also truly afraid of dogs. Her mother had been bitten as a child and had instilled her own fear in her children. When I first met Allison and her mother, Joann, they both stayed away from Sandy. As I tried to explain that Sandy was great and that they would become best friends, Allison started to cry. I decided not to work that day and just talked to them instead. I could see that Joann was rather strict with Allison, and she was very well behaved—but as I continued to watch her, I could also see that Allison had the same streak of mischief as Andrea, which was perfect for the character of Annie.

The next day I took Allison into the rehearsal room without her mother. As we talked, she told me it was tough being the youngest of six kids because everyone bossed her around. And she admitted that everyone in the family was afraid of dogs. I asked her if she'd like to play a dirty trick on everyone. For the first time I saw a little smile and a flicker of interest. Our trick would be that whenever she could she would sneak up behind her mom and scare her with Sandy. Of course, to do that, she would have to learn to train him.

By the end of the hour, Allison was petting Sandy. Within a couple of days, all the love and affection that kids have stored up inside for a pet came rushing out, and she attached to Sandy like glue. And Sandy seemed proud to have a new child showering him with affection. We never told her mom what we were up to, and at the end of the first week, Allison came out of the rehearsal room, snuck up behind her mom, and made Sandy bark. Poor Joann nearly jumped out of her skin. Allison smiled at me, and I knew she had a bond with Sandy that would be very special.

After two and a half years, Allison also grew out of the role, and it was decided that she would be replaced by her understudy, Alyson Kirk. The switch took place in September 1982, but Alyson Kirk didn't get to play the role for long. *Annie* closed in January 1983. At that time, it was the eighth-longest-running show in Broadway history. Sandy went into the record books as the longest-running dog on Broadway. We'd gone to the White House four times, met all sorts of celebrities, and I had written a children's book about Sandy. And although I sometimes was jealous of Sandy's fame, in my heart I knew this was just the first step toward my real career.

For the final show, Martin Charnin invited the producers, managers, designers, and every actor who had ever appeared in *Annie* across the country to attend, so he could bring them onstage one more time. It was very emotional—children were crying, adults were crying. There were about two hundred people when he was done. Even the stagehands came onstage. I remained in my spot in the wings, where I was giving Sandy the hand signal to stay. And then it was over. People were asked to leave the stage, and I was still offstage. Andrea, Shelley, Sarah, Allison, and Alyson all came offstage, angry that after seven years on this show, Martin had forgotten to thank me. As I looked at those five girls who were now young women, I felt a sense of pride that they still cared about Sandy and me.

The only two left onstage were Martin and Tom Meehan, the writer of *Annie*. They had prepared a little script. Martin said, "You know, Tom, maybe we should do a sequel." And Tom replied, "Yes—we could call it *Annie 2*." And in that moment of intense emotion, with the five young ladies who had played Annie all standing around me, I thought, *Oh no—here we go again*.

I also realized that Norma Terris had been right—Sandy had learned to trust me and I had learned to trust him. I had learned so much from him. After the show became successful, I tried to repay the money she had loaned me. She refused, saying her repayment was knowing this dog would be cared for—for the rest of his life. For the entire run of *Annie*—and beyond—Sandy was my closest companion. We had become a team. There were only a handful of nights when he did not sleep next to me, and even when I had to go and do other shows, he was still waiting at home each night, happy to see me.

The longest-running dog on Broadway.
Photo by Michael Carr

There were so many times we were asked to do a new behavior for a show or appearance. And each time I would sit with him quietly, and we would figure out a way to make that happen. I enjoyed every second of it, and I hoped it would never end.

Chapter 3

Camelot's Horrid

With the success of *Annie* and the touring company that was on the road, 1979 was a great year. The only thing that could have made it better would have been another Broadway show—and that's exactly what happened.

One of the production stage managers for *Annie* was Jerry Adler. He was a big, fatherly type, very loving, and got along with everybody. To him I was just "the kid." Jerry had many years of experience, but he was the type who came into a show, stayed for a while, then was always moving on to the next thing. He soon left *Annie* to take over a revival of the musical *Camelot*. What made this production special was that Richard Burton was coming back to re-create his role as King Arthur. Alan Jay Lerner, who wrote the original book and lyrics, was going to be involved in updating the production. In late 1979 Jerry gave me a call and said, "I'm doing this show, and I want you on it, kid. We need a sheepdog to walk onstage and sit there, do nothing, and then walk off."

Now, prior to *Annie*, no one thought you could train a dog to be a character in a Broadway musical, or in any stage event for that matter. Before Sandy appeared in *Annie*, most shows that used animals used them as props or sight gags. In *Camelot*, King Arthur has a friend named King Pellinore, a confused but comical character who owns an Old English

Paxton Whitehead, as King Pellinore, with Bob in the revival of *Camelot. Photo by Martha Swope,*
© New York Public Library for the Performing Arts

sheepdog named Horrid. Pellinore is always getting lost and relying on Horrid to help him find his way. The joke, of course, is that a sheepdog has a lot of hair over its eyes and can't see where it's going, so Horrid is always leading Pellinore in the wrong direction.

So, could I do it again? Could I get another dog to perform onstage and make the same magic? I started my search through the pounds of New York City, New Jersey, and Connecticut. Now, Old English sheepdogs are herding dogs. They have thick coats to protect them from the elements, and they're very high-energy—they need a lot of exercise and a lot of grooming. Sometimes they can be good with families, but sometimes, when their predatory instinct comes out, they're not so good with children and other small creatures. Most of the sheepdogs that I was hearing about were the bad ones. They had bitten someone or were out of control or too wild.

By now I was very popular with the animal shelters in the New York City area because whenever I could I would bring Sandy to help out with publicity for the cause of homeless animals. So I was able to call the shelters in the area and ask them to help me find a certain type of dog. The Associated Humane Society in Newark, New Jersey, called me back and said they had a big sheepdog mix that they thought was very calm, very quiet, and that would be good for the show.

The Associated Humane Society is the central animal rescue group for Newark, so it gets a lot of strays. I was met by the assistant executive director, Roseann Trezza, who gave me a tour, then led me to the back. At the end of an outdoor run was a big, wet, grayish, hairy thing she called "Bob"— three and a half years old, owner surrendered, very sweet. As we opened the door, he slowly turned his head and lumbered over to us. He had to be one of the ugliest dogs I had ever seen in my life. He was probably about 70 or 80 pounds, with a long, pink nose and bald patches on his body. Unlike the beautiful pedigree sheepdogs you see in books or Disney movies, Bob's hair was thin and stringy, and he had a tail—not something you see in that breed. And this was a little ratlike tail, with no hair on it at all. He was a sight, but I was immediately struck by the fact that he lumbered over, sat down, leaned against me, and looked up at me with these big brown eyes. I couldn't resist him.

I stood back and looked at him and asked why his coat was so bad. Their guess was probably poor diet and being exposed to the elements, but with a little love and affection and some proper treatment, we could make him look better. I put a leash on him and took him for a walk, and he didn't pull me down the street. Although he wasn't a true sheepdog, I thought that with the right grooming, he'd be even funnier onstage because of his skinny, hairless tail. So I decided to adopt Bob.

Finding an understudy was not as easy. Again, as I looked through the shelters, most of the dogs I saw were aggressive. Then I visited an animal control agency in another New Jersey town where a dog had been turned in because she was "too much work." She was a beautiful specimen, with gorgeous long hair. She was smaller than Bob, only about 65 pounds, but she was like a tornado. She was one of those dogs that never stop moving, always twirling around, easily distracted. She was sweet with people, sweet with other dogs, just very high-energy. Her name was Daisy, and I decided to adopt her, too. Within a month, we had the two dogs we were going to use on the show.

I waited a month before I brought Bob and Daisy in to meet Jerry and the rest of the team because I wanted to make him look as presentable as possible. Even after a month he was still a mess. So when I walked Bob into the room, everybody's jaw just sort of dropped, and then they laughed.

Daisy's glamour shot.
Photo by Anita Shevett

They all agreed he was perfect. Bob had passed his audition and was going to be in the show, and Daisy would be the understudy.

Having gotten the dog out of the way, I was very worried about who I would send out with the tour. I had made up this method of training, but I couldn't really describe what I did. How could I possibly start interviewing people and explaining the job when I didn't even know how *I* did it? As I started talking to people, people who said they loved dogs or worked in theater or whatever, nobody struck me as having the same feelings I did when it came to being responsible and really caring about the animals. I thought I needed someone with the same kind of background I had. I needed somebody who was family.

Growing up, I had a cousin named Sue Spitzel—we were like brother and sister. We were the best of friends, and we would laugh and have great times together. Sue was living in Santa Cruz, California, when I called her up and offered her the job. At first she thought I was playing a practical joke on her, because that's what we always did. When I kept telling her I was serious, she said, "But Bill, I've never done a professional show or trained a dog. Why do you think I'd be good for this?" The only answer I had was that I knew in my heart she would be. I could teach her the other stuff, but I can't teach people how to be caring and nurturing. After a couple of weeks of coaxing, she said she'd do it.

Now, neither of us had any idea what we were really getting into, but at least I had an idea of what the touring life was like from *Annie*. I had decided that I would never fly my dogs in the baggage compartment of a plane—I thought it was too stressful and too dangerous for dogs that we spent thousands of hours preparing to be in a show. Putting their life and welfare at risk in any way was just something I didn't want to do. For the *Annie* tour, my girlfriend, Jude, was traveling the country with our latest Sandy dog, Moose, in a customized van. We decided to do that for Sue as well. That meant we'd have three vans—the one I used in New York, the one Jude was driving on tour, and now this new one. Things were getting really expensive, so we bought a basic panel van that I would modify myself. I had become pretty good at putting in customized floors, paneling the walls, and adding a little bed in the back. Sue was looking forward to the adventure of traveling the country in this blue van. She moved to New Jersey and lived with me and the dogs. She watched while I trained them so she could see for herself what I did.

When rehearsals began in the spring of 1980, I can remember Sue coming into New York and meeting the cast and seeing everything from an outsider's perspective. Coming from a California "hippie" town, she was amazed at the big egos and all the money that was being spent. We were both middle-class kids, the children of Italian immigrants, amazed to be on Broadway. It was nice to have someone around who looked at show business the same way I did. Plus, Sue has a really warm and loving personality, with a touch of naiveté. She was immediately well liked and quickly made friends with the cast and crew. When the cast saw Bob with his Sad Sack face, they all fell in love with him, too. People would come up and hug him, and he would give them a big sloppy kiss. He was just a wonderful dog to be around.

We rehearsed in New York for five weeks, and then the show moved to Toronto to open the tour. While all the other actors were staying in hotels, we decided to get an apartment so the dogs would have more room for the two months we were setting up and running the show. When the time came, we loaded up the two dogs in our brand-new customized blue van and drove to Canada. I stayed for two weeks, helping to get things set up and making sure Sue and Bob were okay. Once the show was running smoothly, I headed back to New York, but it was exciting to go through the whole process and see the show finally come to fruition.

Bob was a trouper. The first night, he walked out onstage, looked at the audience, and didn't seem to care that they were there. He obeyed his commands, sat for the scene, and walked off. It was probably one of the smoothest transitions into a show that we ever had. The show played its run in Toronto and then came to New York to open at the State Theater in Lincoln Center that summer. Although Richard Burton had started to slow down a bit at this point in his career, no one has ever mastered the words of King Arthur the way he did. He could bring tears to your eyes at every

We clean up pretty well—me and Sue with Bob and Daisy.
Photo by Anita Shevett

performance with the speech about how he pulled the sword from the stone. He was a brilliant actor, but he was also kind and generous to everyone involved in the tour. He gave the cast opening night gifts. He always made sure there was food set up for us when we arrived at the theater. And he would smile and pat Bob on the head while they were waiting backstage.

Bob did a great job for the first eight months of the tour. Christmas that year was spent in San Francisco, with a big party set up at the theater. One of the actors was going to make a surprise entrance dressed up as Santa Claus. Josephine, the wardrobe mistress, custom-fit a pair of old red pajamas for Bob—the kind with the "trapdoor" on the backside, for his tail to poke through. She made him a black patent-leather belt and a Santa's hat. He already had white paws and a big white beard—a perfect Santa (for a dog). On the back of his little suit we put the words SANTA PAWS. Sue had Bob waiting at the bottom of the steps, and, on cue, Santa Claus and Santa Paws ran up the steps together to greet the waiting company. There was a huge roar of laughter and applause. Bob ran over to see Richard Burton, who just laughed. Bob loved parties and people. He would go out the stage door after every performance to be hugged and kissed by his fans, eager to accept the love and praise he deserved.

Soon after Christmas, Bob started to seem tired and lethargic. We thought it was from the touring schedule—until Sue noticed a lump on his neck. We immediately got him to the vet, who did a biopsy. The news was not good: He had a tumor that encapsulated the lymph node. The only way to treat this type of cancer was to remove the lymph node and hope that it hasn't spread. Fortunately, San Francisco had a very famous oncology vet there who worked with us and did the best he could.

We scheduled the surgery for Bob during the first week of January, which meant we'd have to put Daisy on. That sent chills through our spines. While we had worked with Daisy on a limited basis, we all knew that she was easily spooked and easily distracted. For her first performance, we asked an actor playing another knight to take her leash and hold her when she entered with King Pellinore because we knew she probably wouldn't stay still. That first night she was very nervous, always looking around. The knight knelt down and tried to calm her, at which point Daisy decided he should rub her belly and immediately threw herself on her back, all four legs in the air running like crazy, completely upstaging the scene. Everybody in the audience was laughing, and everybody onstage was laughing—not exactly an ideal debut.

After Bob's tumor was removed, there were small sutures on his neck. The doctor felt that he should take ten days off before wearing his collar again, so that's how long Daisy performed for us. During that time Bob would be in the dressing room, and he'd hear his cue and get his leash, but we'd have to tell him it wasn't his time to go to work, and he would get sad and lie down. Bob's incision healed nicely and he started to regain his strength. The night we decided that Bob was going to go back on, Sue said to him, "Do you want to go onstage?—do you want to go onstage?" He jumped right up, tail wagging a mile a minute, and once again went over and grabbed his leash. He dragged Sue to the stage because he was so happy to go on, and everybody was petting him and cheering him on backstage: the stagehands, the actors, and the crew. His feeling of pure happiness quickly spread. Everyone congratulated him, so happy to have him back. He went out and did a perfect show.

About a week later he spiked a fever and was brought back to the vet. I was back home in New Jersey when the vet called me to say the prognosis was not good. It looked like the tumor had spread to other parts of his body, and within a short while he would die a very painful death. This was the first time that I had been forced to deal with the euthanasia issue with any of my performing dogs, although I did have two dogs that died of natural causes. I knew my cousin Sue would be devastated. I knew this dog had done a great job for us and really deserved a long, happy life. But I also knew the kindest thing to do would be to put him to sleep before he got too sick. I had to make the decision.

I decided not to tell Sue what we were going to do. Instead, I told her that she needed to bring him in for some more tests. The vet assured me that he would explain everything to Sue when she got there and help her get through her grief. It's the first time I ever lied to one of my trainers, but I knew it would be the best thing for Bob, and, ultimately, the best thing for Sue.

Sue remembers spending the last few days with him before he went back in. She had been sleeping on the floor with him because he was too big for the bed, hugging him and staying close. They went for a long, slow walk. She remembers bringing him to the vet's office, where they told her what they were going to do. She remembers hugging him and crying and leaving. She didn't want Bob to suffer, either. Bob had become her dog. She fell apart—and then had to go back and tell the cast, who were very sad.

Canine Star treatment.
Photo by Anita Shevett

Bob was a member of the company as much as anyone else, and when anyone in a show is hurt, everyone shares a ripple of sadness.

After Bob's death we had another month and a half in San Francisco. I started looking for another understudy dog back East in the New York area. Sue got a lot of rehearsal time in the theater so Daisy could start getting used to working onstage, and she got much better. I got nightly reports, and I was amazed at how well she did. I felt, in my heart, that Daisy knew Sue was very sad, and one of the few times Sue would feel better was when Daisy performed well, so she rose to the occasion.

After San Francisco, the tour went to Los Angeles. While there, Richard Burton fell ill. During a performance he suddenly wasn't able to sing or dance one of the numbers. They brought down the curtain, and after a delay, the show continued with the understudy. Burton didn't perform the role again. They were able to persuade Richard Harris, who had played Arthur in the film version of *Camelot*, to take over the rest of the tour. In less than a month Bob had passed away and we had also lost our human star. Harris was a wonderful actor, but he never had the same relationship with the cast and crew that Burton did. Instead of it being a family, it just felt like a job.

I found another dog, named Boy, to understudy Daisy, and the tour continued. The show played St. Louis, Minneapolis, Boston, and Washington, and then in October the show went back to Broadway and opened at the Winter Garden Theater for a limited run. The show was filmed there for Home Box Office. Sue left after that. Even though the tour continued, her heart wasn't in it after the loss of Bob. Another of my trainers, Jim Crosley, took over.

While the sheepdogs would have been welcome to stay with me after the tour, I felt that their energy and their personalities were better suited to be in homes where they were the only dogs. We placed Daisy with a police officer in northern New Jersey who had had sheepdogs before and was looking for a new one. Boy, the understudy, found a home in North Carolina, where he could run through the woods and get plenty of exercise, rather than being cooped up in city hotel rooms anymore.

Sue and I still talk about that tour, and we remember it with smiles and tears, because we're really remembering Richard Burton and Bob the sheepdog.

Chapter 4

Frankenstein's Revenge

In 1980, famed theatrical owner and producer Jimmy Nederlander was producing a new play based on Mary Shelley's *Frankenstein*. The concept: an updated version with special effects never before seen on Broadway—a "scary show" that would frighten and delight audiences. The scenic designer, Douglas Schmidt, was given carte blanche to build a set that would defy belief. They got famed puppeteer Bil Baird and his son, Peter, to build lifelike puppets of the creature and Dr. Frankenstein, all to thrill the audience. The playwright, Vic Gianella, added some elements to make the story even scarier. He expanded the role of Frankenstein's younger brother—a part often omitted in movie versions of the book. The boy and his dog would eventually be killed by the creature. Because of the dark subject matter, they hired a young actor named Scotty Schwartz, who was actually eleven at the time, to play the six-year-old brother. (A medical condition limited his growth, so he really did look that young.)

When the Nederlander office called me to set up a meeting for the new show, I was flabbergasted. At this point, I thought I had been lucky once with Sandy—I was a kid from Connecticut with no dog-training background who happened to train the most famous dog in Broadway history.

Jill P. Rose and Scott Schwartz with Fritz in *Frankenstein*. *Photo by Martha Swope, © New York Public Library for the Performing Arts*

I was sure I was a one-hit wonder—I didn't really count *Camelot*, since the dogs didn't have to do much onstage. But Jimmy Nederlander thought I was the guy to provide the dogs for this production.

I met the director and the writer and they were very nice. As they explained the concept of the show I got very excited because they had a clear-cut idea to wow an audience. The dog was just an extra bonus. The script was simple: They wanted a calm dog that would hang out with the boy like a family pet in the first act. In the second act, they wanted the dog and the boy to get lost in the woods and get killed by the creature. Who wouldn't get upset over a creature killing an innocent boy and his dog? My question was, How do we depict the dead dog? The director thought I could train the dog to play dead. The answer was yes and no—I could train the dog to play dead, but not eight times a week in front of a live audience. "Can't we use a dummy?" I asked. The director's reaction was, "We have the best puppeteer in the world. He might be able to do it."

When I asked what kind of dog they had in mind, the author said, "A Westie is very cute. Do you have any trained Westies?" At that moment, I didn't know what a Westie was, but with my mind racing, I said I could easily find one. As I said earlier, I was in shock. Respected people in the Broadway community thought of me as an expert. There were lots of animal trainers in New York at the time they could have called, many with long lists of movie credits. But up until then, no one had been able to figure out how to get an animal onstage as a real character. I was beginning to understand that what Sandy and I did had been groundbreaking. I took great pride in that. Plus, I had rescued about six dogs to be in *Annie* and was involved in charity work for shelters around New York, helping to save the lives of countless animals. Now I had the opportunity to be in another hit show and also continue to forward the cause of helping animals. This was a dream come true.

I went to my dog book and looked up Westies. West Highland white terriers are little, long-haired dogs from Scotland that were used as ratters. Like most terriers, they have a very strong prey drive. They're small enough to get into the holes, smart enough to find and kill prey by themselves, and tenacious enough to not give up. Plus, they were hearty little dogs that could withstand the harsh elements of Scotland. How did this breed fit into a play taking place in Germany in the 1800s? I wondered, but never questioned the choice.

I put out the call to my friends at the regional shelters, asking them to look for a Westie. The response was either "What's that?" or "We have never seen a Westie in a shelter." These dogs are pretty rare, so the shelters don't see a lot of them. Plus, the few they had seen were so aggressive, they had to be put to sleep. Remember, terriers were bred to be independent hunters and are not easily trained by inexperienced pet owners. The Sandy dogs were mixed breeds, so it was easy to find dogs with good temperaments. But no one had ever heard of a calm Westie. I was crushed that I wouldn't be able to save a dog from a pound and make it into a star. Outside of Benji, the movie dog who was popular at the time, the public perception was that dogs in shelters were damaged goods. I proved with Sandy that they were just as good as any purebred and wanted to use this opportunity to do it again. But instead, I opted to call the American Kennel Club for breeder recommendations and get one from a responsible breeder. To my surprise, there were very few on the East Coast, but the ones I called were willing to sell me one of their "breeding stock."

This was all new to me. I mean, I paid seven dollars for the original Sandy and adopted all of his understudies. All my childhood dogs were from farm litters or pet shops. How much could a "breeder" cost? To my surprise, I found they would cost hundreds of dollars. I was horrified! How could one full-grown dog cost so much? I soon found out why. Most reputable breeders put many hours and thousands of dollars into their dogs, hoping to win ribbons at major dog shows. If you have a prize-winning male or female, their puppies are the only things that you can sell to recoup those expenses. If they sold me a dog, they would need to make up for the revenue lost by not being able to sell that dog's puppies—hence, the high price.

When I visited the breeders, I could see the care they put into the dogs. But I had a sinking sense of sadness walking through these kennels. I had firsthand experience seeing dogs in shelters, barking and looking unhappy with confinement. Then I went to the breeders and saw rows of dogs in cages whose whole lives were spent being bred for puppies. Even though these kennels were clean, free of disease, air-conditioned, and new, I felt sorry these dogs didn't have a better life. And when I started to go to breeders who were less well known, so-called "backyard breeders," the conditions the dogs were kept in were sometimes no better than what I saw at the animal shelters. This was a side of dog ownership I had never seen and never wanted to be a part of.

Through one of the breeders I got the name of a family who had a middle-aged male dog they were willing to sell cheap. It seems his stud days were over because he was no longer producing offspring. They had a few dogs in their backyard and didn't want the extra expense of keeping him until he died if he wasn't producing. Some gratitude, huh? I called and they seemed very nice, but they lived in North Carolina. And they were asking $600 for him. While that was one week's salary for me from *Annie,* it was cheaper than any other breeder, and the people who knew this dog said he was calm and gentle. So on the day off from *Annie*, I drove down to meet Bubba.

As I went into the family's small kennels, I saw a half-dozen white dogs jumping and barking ferociously. Bubba was sitting in his cage, looking alert. We picked him up and brought him to the porch of the house. He perked right up and was happy to be getting some attention. From all the things they had said, and from his nice quiet disposition, I knew I had found the dog for the show. I paid them the money and they let me stay overnight in their guest room. The next morning Bubba became "Fritz," which was the name of the character in the show. We left early and drove back to do the evening show of *Annie*. Fritz was happy to be going and was no problem.

Fritz fit in perfectly with my other dogs. The creative team liked him, and agreed that he was ideal for the show. About that time I got a call from my friends at the Associated Humane Society in Newark. They said they had a little male Westie, slightly skittish and in poor physical condition, but with a nice temperament. Since I needed an understudy, I raced down to see him. What I saw shocked me. This dog was thin as a skeleton, had stringy hair, and was bald in spots. He was a young dog, about two years old, shy with strangers, but friendly with the shelter people he knew. He was cautious with me, but let me hold him. They called him Snowball. My heart went out to him. While he would probably never be a performing dog, I felt I could help him, so I adopted him. He immediately went to my vet for a complete checkup and remained there for about a week while they cured his intestinal worms.

As Snowy (his new name) began to feel better, his energy improved. He was the direct opposite of Fritz, who was calm and loving. Snowy was a true terrier. He would pick fights with the bigger dogs that challenged him, he barked at everything, and he never sat still except for sleeping. But it was a joy to see him come back to life and good health, and he got along with Fritz.

Rehearsal began as scheduled, and I was thrilled to be part of this new project. The cast was brilliant. The design team had cooked up an unbelievable set. The director and writer had a clear vision of what they wanted, and it seemed flawless. I spent my days with the dogs in rehearsal, getting used to the action and the cast and working individually with Scotty Schwartz.

One of the most interesting things I've ever done in my career is work with puppeteer Bil Baird, who was given the job of making the dead "Fritz." When I first met him he looked exactly like you'd picture a puppeteer. He was white haired with a white beard and looked like Gepetto from *Pinocchio*. He was soft spoken and kind. He measured Fritz from every angle and went to work. When he came back with the finished puppet, it was incredible. He used white yak hair to simulate the white Westie fur. The puppet had enough movable joints so that when you carried it, it moved exactly like a limp body. The detail was incredible in the face, even down to the tongue, which hung out and had glycerin drops on it to look like saliva. It was a masterpiece and even fooled the dogs when they first saw it!

We were slated to open the show in New York at the famed Palace Theater. The tech rehearsals in this show went on longer than any show I had worked on. We spent weeks in the theater going from scene to scene. The show opened with a blizzard onstage and Dr. Frankenstein and the creature scaling a mountain. The scene went black, and in seven seconds, we were in the drawing room of the Frankenstein estate with Scotty, the dog, and four other actors onstage. It was an incredible effect, accomplished by a large white silk drape covering the set with everyone preset underneath, and two life-sized Bil Baird puppets being controlled from behind the set. The lights would go down and the silk would be pulled into a hole at center stage. And that was only the beginning. The laboratory scene had electricity, bubbles, and, of course, the creature, who was lifted up into the air on a table and struck by lightning. The creature himself was scary to look at and required two hours of makeup. And in the end, the entire lab would blow up and collapse around the actors, only to be covered again by the white silk to reenact the opening scene in the blizzard. They even pulled out seats in the audience and put huge speakers in the floor so that when the thunder and lightning crashed, the entire orchestra area would vibrate. It was a feat unmatched in theater design.

During all the waiting around, we would sit and listen to the legendary actor John Carradine, who was playing a small part in the play. Because of his age, John only came to rehearsal for his one scene. He was very professional and quiet. During these long hours at the theater, he would hold court and tell stories of the old days. He'd tell us about John Barrymore and his drinking escapades, or about working with Boris Karloff and Bela Lugosi. He was a treasure to be around.

We began previews on December 9—it was such a thrill to say I had two shows running on Broadway at the same time. Fritz was doing great.

He was perfectly calm under the big white drape in the opening. He played with Scotty and went off, part of a perfect serene picture. In the second act, the family is having a picnic. Fritz wanders across the stage into the woods, to where we know the creature is hiding. We hear an offstage cry, and the creature carries in the puppet dog and puts it right on the edge of the stage, where the audience can get a good look at it. Scotty comes in, sees his dog hurt, and gets upset. As the creature tries to calm him, he kills the boy, too. It was very effective.

During previews, the writer and director decided Fritz's calm disposition wouldn't prompt the creature to hurt him. They asked if Fritz could run offstage as if he were attacking something. While it made sense, it was hard to do. I had searched for a dog that was very calm so he wouldn't upstage the action. Fritz rarely got excited about anything, and that's what made him perfect for the first-act scenes.

So each day during rehearsals, I tried toys, balls, every food from Milk-Bones to steak, but the most he would do was get center stage and then trot toward the wings. I was at a loss. I couldn't find anything in his daily life with me that would make him run. And the director was politely asking when I would make it work because it would really help the scene. I was stumped. Then one day I saw my friend Mary Lee walking her dog. It was a little black poodle named Fleur, and she had a diaper on. I asked why, and Mary Lee said Fleur was in heat, and it was the only way to keep the apartment clean.

"Monster? What monster?"

Then it hit me. What was the one thing Fritz had done well all his life? Be a stud. So I asked Mary Lee to bring Fleur to the theater. I made her my assistant and put her stage right. I went up and got Fritz and gave him to the stage manager, stage left. On cue I had them release Fritz, with Mary holding Fleur behind the curtain next to me. When Fritz hit center stage, I called his name, and when he looked, I pulled the curtain back. There he saw Mary holding this little black poodle. He took one sniff and ran to her like a bat out of hell. At the moment he hit the wings, I sent Mary Lee and Fleur one way and I grabbed Fritz and went in the other direction. I said to him, "Sorry, buddy, you missed her. Maybe you'll get her tomorrow night." The director and writer were thrilled. When I told them how we did it, they couldn't believe it. For the rest of the run it worked perfectly. Fleur was soon out of heat, but it didn't matter. Fritz was determined he was going to get that girl one day, and he kept on trying.

The next night, a half-hour before the curtain went up, I was called to the stage door. An officer from the American Society for the Prevention of Cruelty to Animals (ASPCA) stood there—a very large man, in full uniform with badge and gun—asking to speak to the animal trainer. I said, "That's me." He said, "We've received complaints about a dog being drugged in this show, and we're here to investigate."

"Drugged?" I said. "We would never drug an animal."

"Well, the complaint says that someone has tranquilized a dog," the officer said.

All of a sudden it made sense to me. It only took a few seconds for Fritz to walk offstage and the creature to enter with the puppet. Animal lovers must have thought the only way to make it happen was to drug the dog. I started to laugh, and I told the officer the story. He did not laugh. We worked it out with the stage manager to show him the puppet. While he was intrigued, he said he still had to see the scene in question to make sure no animals were being harmed. So now I had to handle a poodle in heat, Fritz, and an ASPCA officer to make sure no one got hurt, all at the same time. Once the officer had watched the scene, he thanked me for being so cooperative and said he would write up his report.

We thought it was over and done with until the next night, when he was there again. This time he was more apologetic but said another complaint had been filed, so he had to come back. He was a little more talkative and wanted to know more about the show. I introduced him to the cast, and he got a big kick out of it. The third night he came to the stage door and asked me to say he had been there the whole night. There was another complaint and he wanted to get home. We shook hands and he assured me that after three observations, they could now close the case. Our creators loved the fact that the audience was so in tune with the play.

This was the first time that I really understood the power of animals onstage. I had always been amazed at the positive reaction to Sandy and my other dogs—but here we were showing an animal being mistreated. Instead of understanding it was just a play, the audience was concerned about the welfare of the animal. It was a great lesson for me in two ways: It reinforced that I needed to be able to prove we always did things humanely. It also showed me that the audience's reaction to animals onstage is much stronger than what they would feel watching a movie or a television show.

Audiences that were coming to see the show in previews loved it, and the word of mouth was great. The show scared the pants off you. Because of the audience reaction, we were sure it was going to be a hit. One of the producers was the famed restaurateur, Joe Kipness, who planned a lavish opening party. We even had our wardrobe department make two little black tuxedos for the Westies. They looked so cute.

Opening night was a black-tie affair, just like old Broadway. The audience loved the show, and we had to take eleven standing ovations. It was incredible—the audience would not stop clapping. We went to the party on cloud nine. Everyone waited anxiously for the reviews. As the papers started coming in around midnight, the mood changed. The first review was bad. The second was worse. And the *New York Times* was worst of all. The major complaint was that the creative team had taken this piece of classic literature and turned it into a horror show. They took a highbrow stance on how the story was changed for a few cheap thrills. The critics obviously didn't look around at what the audience was doing during the curtain calls.

While it looked bad, the cast was hopeful. Our other producer, Terry Allen Kramer, made it clear she planned to make it work. We'd do an advertising campaign and ignore the critics. But the next day when I went to the theater, there was a crew ripping out our beautiful scenery and putting it in the trash. It seems the Nederlanders wanted their rental money up front because of the poor reviews. Terry tried to persuade them to give her a break, but they wanted it that day or else. She couldn't meet the deadline. It was a cold-blooded thing to do, and we couldn't understand it. We finally figured out the reason soon after that. It seems that at the same time we were opening, a new musical was getting rave reviews on the road. The show was waiting for a New York theater to become available, and the star was very interested in playing the Palace. The theater owners saw our bad reviews as an excuse to bring in a musical that would make them a lot more money than a play, and they took it. A week after they threw our set out on the street, *Woman of the Year* moved in, with Lauren Bacall making her first Broadway appearance in nearly twenty years. And they were right—*Woman of the Year* was a big hit, ran for a long time, and made a lot of money.

Fritz and Snowy were out of a job before they knew it. The sad thing was, they had really enjoyed the experience of being loved by all those people—especially Snowy. The writer, Vic Gianella, took a particular interest in Snowy because he was the underdog, and Fritz got all the attention. After it was over, I saw Vic, and in passing he said he wished he could have Snowy. I said, "You want him?" He said, "Could I?" And I reassured him that I could think of no better home for this dog. It was love at first sight and the least I could do for the man. Snowy lived a very full and healthy life. Vic stayed in touch over the years and let me know when Snowy died. Before all the props were thrown away, Vic got to the theater and salvaged that beautiful puppet dog Bil Baird had made. He kept it on the top of his couch and would often freak out his friends by pretending that it was Snowy.

Fritz was too good a soul to send back to the breeder. He was perfect for someone who needed a quiet dog. Around that time my mother's dog passed away of old age. Even though she and my dad swore no more dogs, I conveniently made an excuse for them to babysit Fritz, and after that, he never came home to me again, the first of many "show" dogs and cats they adopted. He was the best pet. He would ride in the front baskets of my parents' bikes and soon became a local celebrity. He made his daily rounds, getting treats from all of their friends. He did a few more commercials and print jobs for me, and lived a long and happy life.

Chapter 5

Black Cats Are Bad Luck

Annie was such a big hit that they started preparing for national tours in 1978, and Simon & Schuster even asked me to write a book about Sandy. That summer the producers asked me if I would be interested in training the dogs for the first and second national companies. Now with Sandy, I had just made it all up as I went along, and the prospect of doing it again with a different dog was a little scary, but I was very interested.

At the time, I was being represented by one of the big New York animal agencies. They helped negotiate my new contract and were taking 15 percent of all my earnings. They were trainers themselves, and, as I quickly learned, having my competitors negotiate for me was not a very good idea. As the summer progressed, I was writing my book *Sandy: The Autobiography of a Star,* and thinking about rescuing dogs for the tours. I kept talking to our general managers about when I was going to be able to start. In September I asked again and was told that my agents had said I wasn't qualified to do the road companies—so the general managers had hired them instead of me.

I felt betrayed both by the show and my agents. I was in the theater because I loved it, and I thought people would genuinely support my work.

David Alan Grier, as Jackie Robinson, in *The First*. *Photo by Martha Swope, © New York Public Library for the Performing Arts*

Plus, the fact that the producers had agreed to hire another animal trainer made me doubt my abilities. I subsequently fired my agents and received all my back commissions. I started to think about going back to acting and forgetting all about animal training. Maybe *Annie* had been a one-time deal with a special dog. But soon after that I was asked to work on *Camelot* and *Frankenstein,* so by 1981, I had three Broadway credits to my name. It seemed I was slowly building a reputation for my ability to train animals for live theater.

One person who always had faith in me was Martin Charnin, the creator and director of *Annie*. He had written the lyrics for a new musical based on the book and movie *I Remember Mama.* Martin asked me to train a cat for this show. Still feeling somewhat doubtful about my credentials and my expertise, I turned him down. I said, "Martin, I really don't know anything about cats. They're difficult animals to train. I've had cats, but they don't really listen to people." They ultimately contacted my old agents, but from what I've been told, the cat they provided didn't work out, and they ended up using a stuffed cat in the production. The next time Martin came to me was when he asked me to train the dogs for the third and fourth national companies of *Annie* because he was unhappy with the job done on the first and second companies, and he felt I could do it right. I've always been grateful to Martin for being the first to trust me and give me the chance to demonstrate my talents to the Broadway community.

In September 1981 I was again contacted by *Annie*'s general managers because they were representing Martin's new musical *The First*—the story of Jackie Robinson. It was a baseball musical about breaking the color barrier and accepting people for who they are. Martin was born and raised in New York City, and Jackie Robinson had been one of his heroes when he was growing up. As they were conceiving the musical in rehearsals, they decided they needed a very strong finish to the end of the first act, when Jackie Robinson takes the field for the first time at Ebbets Field. Historically, the crowd booed and jeered. Knowing that Jackie Robinson was very superstitious, someone in the stands threw a black cat onto the field, where it died. Despite all that, Jackie Robinson played the game and became one of the all-time greats.

They decided to have David Alan Grier, the young, unknown actor from Yale who was playing Jackie Robinson, come center stage. We hear the crowd boo, jeer, and shout racial slurs. The writers decided that it would be amazing to have a real black cat land on the stage as the curtain came down—a brilliant idea. Martin came to me again, knowing that I was now successfully providing the dogs for the new *Annie* road companies. His confidence in me, and the recognition I was receiving from other Broadway directors and producers, made me think I should give this a try. All I had to do was figure out how to train a cat.

I took the same approach that I had taken with Sandy and fell back on the experiences I had with animals as a kid. My mother loves cats, so we always had them when I was growing up. I remembered that the cats were very independent. They were friendly, but if you called them, they usually ran the other way. If you picked them up, they would stay with you a little while, and then get off your lap. They didn't show any desire to do anything for humans, except at feeding time. I remembered how, no matter where they were, they would come running when they heard the can opener. Then they would rub against my mother's legs, demanding their food. I thought this was the one thing a cat could be counted on to do—come when it was feeding time. The question was, could I find a cat that would be motivated to do that eight times a week, on a stage, in a Broadway theater, in front of 1,500 people?

True to my promise that I would always try to use rescued animals in shows, I went back to the best resource I had—the animal shelters in and around New York City. I was looking for a cat that was very outgoing, that was sure of himself, and that would want to eat every night at the same time. When I called my friends at the shelters and told them what I was looking for, they really thought I had lost my mind. But with all the goodwill that I had given to these shelters, people were willing to let me look. While I had thought that shelter dogs had a poor life, I was really saddened by the state of the cats—thousands and thousands of kittens being born wild because people didn't spay and neuter their cats. Cats that were emaciated, cats that were frightened, cats that were sick, cats that had been abused—and, at that time, much less likely to be adopted than dogs. In and around the New York City area, I was able to view 200 cats in a day.

At the American Society for the Prevention of Cruelty to Animals in New York I found exactly what I was looking for—a black cat that came right to the front of the cage and wasn't afraid of strangers. He was a very large tomcat that might have been someone's pet at one time, because he was somewhat domesticated, not wild. He was slightly emaciated, so I knew that he was probably very hungry. I took him out of the cage and brought him into the examining room. He stood purring on the examining table, being petted. I opened a can of cat food and he dove in with a ferocious appetite. I thought this cat might work, so I adopted him and called him Champ.

I had been called at the beginning of September, knowing the first preview performance was in mid-October. There was no sense bringing this cat to rehearsal and getting him used to the actors because he would only be interacting with one person onstage. There was no reason to get him used to the company and all of the commotion of the singing and dancing. I decided to wait until the week before we actually got into the real theater to bring the cat in. Meanwhile, I brought him home and set him up in one of my bedrooms so he didn't have to deal with the dogs. Each night I would feed him on a stool. Before I fed him, I would put him on the stool, take a little piece of his cat food, and throw it from the stool onto the floor about three feet away. He would jump down to get it and then come back up. So we created a game where before he got his full meal, he would jump off the stool to chase a little piece of food.

About a week after I'd adopted Champ, I brought him into a rehearsal hall in New York City. Martin loved my idea: I was going to be in the wings with my stool, and at the right moment, I would throw a piece of food onstage. The cat would leap about four or five feet to get it, just as the curtain was coming down. We hoped that it would have the desired effect. A week before the previews started, we went in for tech rehearsals. I asked for a quiet time onstage when the actors weren't there, just to get the cat used to the theater, and they graciously granted me the time.

Now, there's one thing I know for sure—there's no sure thing with an animal. Even though this cat had done this behavior perfectly in the confines of my home, the theater was a very large space. I didn't want him getting spooked, running and getting hurt by the scenery, or crawling out into the audience. I had a black collar on him that matched his fur, and then I got a little piece of fishing line so that he would always be leashed but the audience wouldn't be able to see it. Every day during the supper hour, I would go in and try to teach the cat to get his food. Champ did very well, just like at home—he was hungry, he did his bit, and at the end he got his full meal and was very happy. The first time we tried it with David Alan Grier, the sets, the lights, and the sounds of people yelling and booing confused Champ a little, but by dress rehearsal he was doing it perfectly.

The night of our first preview was very exciting. We had a great cast, a great musical, and a subject that we all believed in. As the first act came to a close, David Alan Grier came center stage—Jackie Robinson was taking his rightful place on the baseball field. We heard the jeers and the slurs. We heard a voice over the speakers shout, "Hey, Jackie, here's something for you," and that was my cue to throw the piece of meat onstage. It worked perfectly. The curtain came down, and I picked up Champ and brought him back to the dressing room where he happily ate his meal. We had accomplished the job. I had trained my first cat for a Broadway show, and it was exciting. We did it the next night and it was successful. I was thrilled—until I had my second brush with law enforcement. The next night, a half-hour before the curtain went up, I was called to the stage door, and there was the same officer who had investigated us on *Frankenstein*. He was asking to speak with the animal trainer. I looked at him and said, "Remember me?"

"Oh no, not you again," he said. "We received complaints that a cat is being abused in this show and they sent me here to investigate—seems I have a reputation in the department for liking Broadway shows."

"You know I would never abuse an animal," I said.

"I didn't know it was you," he said. "The complaint says that someone has been throwing a cat onstage."

This was something we hadn't counted on. By the end of the first act, the audience was already so emotionally involved with the character and the plot that no one expected to see a cat fly out onto the stage. Because it was so quick, they didn't know where Champ came from, and they were assuming he had been thrown from a great height. People thought someone had actually thrown a cat onstage in the same way that they had during Jackie Robinson's first appearance at Ebbets Field.

I invited the officer in, got him a cup of coffee, and explained to him, while the stage manager was there, exactly what we were doing. While he understood, met the cat, and saw the situation, he said he still had to actually witness the performance so that he could put in a report that no animals were being abused. He stood behind me in the wings, saw me bring Champ out, put on the safety line, then do the behavior just as the curtain came down. This time he laughed. He thought we had handled it perfectly and didn't understand why people thought we were hurting cats. He would write it up in his report that no cats were abused and said he would probably see us soon. Two nights later he was back at the stage door, having received another complaint from a patron who felt that cats were being abused in the production. He seemed to like talking to the chorus girls on this show. So, for the second time he watched as we did the same behavior, thanked us very much for the coffee, and went back to the ASPCA.

By the end of the first week, it was apparent we needed to make a change. Although the incident was historically true, that one behavior was hurting the play by shifting the focus from Jackie Robinson to the cat. Martin and the writers decided they had to cut it, and I understood. After that, as the first-act curtain came down at each performance, a stagehand threw a fake watermelon onstage from a ladder in the wings. It had the desired effect—the audience was appalled by the action.

I thought *The First* was a wonderful show but ahead of its time in the way it addressed discrimination. Audiences weren't ready for it, not as part of a musical. The show closed after thirty-seven performances. I was thankful to work on *The First* for many reasons. First, it was another chance to work with Martin Charnin, my mentor. He gave me my start and the confidence that if I put my mind to it, I could do amazing things with animals. And it was another chance to rescue an animal from a shelter and give him a better life. Champ's Broadway career may have been short, but he lived happily with me for many more years and did many more photo shoots.

Chapter 6

Who Are You Calling a Pig?

Camelot closed at the beginning of January 1982. *Annie* was in its sixth year on Broadway. I had the third and fourth national touring companies of *Annie* out and three Broadway credits to my name. But I decided I wanted to expand my business to do more television and movies, so I needed a New York address. I rented an apartment two doors down from the Alvin Theater on West 52nd Street. That's where I established William Berloni Theatrical Animals. Going into the fall of 1982, I had high hopes for new shows and new projects.

Then I heard there was going to be a revival of *Alice in Wonderland*. It was being directed by one of the theater world's most famous actresses, Eva Le Gallienne. She had produced, directed, and appeared in the original production in 1932, and now, fifty years later, she was directing and appearing in a production—at the age of eighty-three. From my research, I knew the production had both a pig and a cat in it, so I contacted the general managers to see if we could put a bid in on the show. They were pleased to hear from us; we went into negotiations and eventually got the job to provide the animals.

The show was slated to open in December, and we finalized the agreements on November 1. Because the show was a revival and was geared

Kate Burton, as Alice, with Hamletta in *Alice in Wonderland*. *Photo by Martha Swope, © New York Public Library for the Performing Arts*

toward a children's audience, they wanted to do as much publicity as possible. The public relations firm decided that they wanted to hold a pig audition in New York City, and they asked me to participate. I found it odd that we were actually going to be auditioning pigs when I had the contract to provide the pig, but their job was to get publicity, and if they had to stretch the truth a little bit, they said they didn't mind.

At first I resisted. I didn't want to lie to the public—I've never lied to the public. The PR firm kept insisting that if I didn't participate in this pig audition, or supervise it, or at the very least *pretend* I was involved, I would be let go from the show. The audition was scheduled for the end of November, and they were going to invite people to come in with their pigs. My first thought was, not only was it untruthful, it would be dangerous because there were plenty of people out there who would show up in New York City with their large and small pigs. There was a stress factor for the animals, a safety factor for the humans, and a hygiene problem. I kept trying to explain that inviting the public was a risky thing. So I said, "Well, then, why don't we stage it from beginning to end?" At that point it was either stage a pig audition or lose the show completely, and because I was trying to build my reputation as the only animal trainer on Broadway, I decided to do it.

In my research, I started looking for pig farmers and 4-H club members in the tri-state area who might be raising pigs in the middle of winter and might be willing to let us use one of their pigs. This was one of those times when going to a shelter wouldn't be possible. There were a lot of farms in New Jersey, Connecticut, and New York, and all of them were raising pigs for slaughter. As we started calling around, a lot of farmers would laugh at us and hang up—nobody believed we were seriously looking for a baby pig to be trained for a Broadway show. Then I got in touch with the 4-H club of Hunterdon County, New Jersey. When I told them what we were doing, they were thrilled to participate because they had a bunch of kids who were raising piglets, and this would be a good opportunity for them to learn more about handling their animals.

I came up with the idea of creating a small, penlike area in the rehearsal studio where we were holding the audition. We got plywood and built a

1-foot-high barrier that was about 20 feet by 20 feet. We got the members of the 4-H club to come in—each owner would have a story about why he was auditioning his pig. The kids were going to pretend they didn't know each other. But before we did that, I had to contact the City of New York because public health laws prohibit livestock from coming into the city unless they have health certificates. This was my first experience calling the city to get a permit for exhibition. We had to verify that all the piglets were vaccinated before we received a permit to do the exhibition.

The show was thrilled. We had eight contestants, and we knew that all the piglets were vaccinated and well cared for. The day came, and the publicity surrounding the event was outstanding. There was television, newspaper, and magazine coverage from all over the world. We held the audition, judged by Kate Burton, who was starring as Alice, Miss Le Gallienne, and me. The young pig who won the part was named Michelle, raised by eight-year-old Vanessa Bolbowlby. Vanessa's family agreed that we could use her piglet for the show. The cameras clicked and the cameras rolled. Not only were we featured in the local papers, the story went out all around the world. They couldn't have asked for a better publicity event to kick off the show in a very fun and light-hearted way. Before we even went into rehearsals we were heroes.

Now, the trouble with pigs is that when they're first born they weigh about 6 or 7 pounds, but they grow rather quickly. By the time they're a month old, they get to be about 30 pounds. That meant the piglet would not last too long because in the show Kate Burton had to be able to walk onstage with the piglet in her arms and say 30 seconds' worth of dialogue; then she'd put the piglet down and it would run offstage. When we started with Michelle, the pig, she was only six days old, but by the time we got into rehearsal she was thirteen days old and growing fast.

The problem was how do we teach a pig to be carried out onstage and then come offstage in the same place every night, in front of an audience? When you pick up baby pigs they squeal. They do not like to be touched, they do not like to be held, they have a very low center of gravity, and so when you pick them up, they become very nervous. And the second part of it was, when we put the pig down, how would she know to come offstage to us?

Well, as we had this baby pig, we had to wean her from her mother, which meant that every four hours we had to bottle-feed her. She was living in our kitchen in New Jersey with the dogs, who thought she was the oddest creature you could imagine. Then we brought her into our apartment, which

Another hungry actor.

happened to be our new office on 52nd Street, across the street from the theater. Of course, when we signed our lease, it said we could have dogs. It didn't say anything about having a pig, so we would sneak her into the apartment every day in a small dog carrier.

By watching her, I learned that—just like clockwork—Michelle got hungry every four hours and would start looking for us to feed her. Piglets are just little eating machines—because their bodies are growing so fast, they need lots of nutrition. The one thing that we could depend on was for her to always be hungry. As soon as I got her bottle ready and started to shake it, she would come running—nothing would stop her from getting that bottle.

Both the pig farmers and the vets said that we had to be careful to keep the bottle level when we fed her, because if you held it up too high, the liquid would go down into her lungs and she would drown. So when we gave her a bottle, we'd keep it level and allow her to suck about half of it down furiously. Then we would take it away from her to give her a chance to swallow, relax, and calm down. Then we would feed her the other half. Well, just like any other baby getting warm milk, once she had her bottle, she got a milk buzz—that warm, fuzzy feeling where she would just close her eyes halfway and digest her food a little bit. Then, in a little while, she would sort of root around for more, and we'd give her the other half. Watching her, I thought we might just have a chance of doing both behaviors.

When we started rehearsing, we timed everything so that by eight o'clock each night, we'd be feeding her one of her bottles. In the wings, right before she went on, we would give her half the bottle. As soon as she finished half, we would hand her to Kate Burton, who would carry her out onstage. Michelle would go out quietly, sort of smacking her lips, eyes closed just long enough for Kate to be able to say her 30 seconds' worth of dialogue. By then I had tied jingle bells to her bottle so that every time I fed her, I would shake the bells and she would come running. So right on cue, when Kate would finish her line, I would shake the jingle bells, and Michelle would wake up and run offstage for the rest of her bottle. It worked like a charm. We had found a way to train our little pig to do the behaviors that we needed just by observing what she was doing.

Now the script also called for a little black kitten, and that was much more difficult. Despite my success with getting a cat to jump onstage in *The First*, I still believed there was no such thing as a trained cat. In *The First*, Champ simply had to jump after a bit of food and then the curtain came down. Here, the cat would be onstage much longer—between the lights, the orchestra, and the audience, I was sure it would run away and hide. So, even though the script called for a kitten, I thought that if I could find a smaller black cat to do the role, that would give us a better chance of success. I visited the local shelters, looking at black cats, but most of them were either too active, too sick, or too old.

At the American Society for the Prevention of Cruelty to Animals we found a tiny black cat that had been a stray. She was healthy, but she was a scaredy-cat. She hung back in her cage and didn't move because she was overwhelmed by all of the goings-on at the shelter. When you opened the door she didn't try to run away, she didn't try to bite you—she just balled up smaller and tried to figure out a way to have you ignore her. When you picked her up, she would curl up in your arms and just sit there, very quiet. I thought this cat had a chance to work, so we adopted her. We named her Ophelia because we had changed our pig's name to Hamletta, our little acting pig. So now we had Hamletta and Ophelia, two great Shakespearean animal actors.

The show opened with Kate Burton and Ophelia sitting on a chair in a living room. When Kate began saying her lines, she would put Ophelia down on the chair. As she went through the looking glass, the chair would be pulled offstage. Just as I had hoped, Ophelia sat quietly with Kate on the chair. Then, when the chair began to move, she would curl into a ball and stay put. At the end of the play, when Alice returned from Wonderland, the chair would ride back out onstage with Ophelia on it. Without fail, both Hamletta and Ophelia performed their roles perfectly in the show.

Because the animals really needed to learn their behaviors onstage, we didn't begin rehearsing until December with the rest of the cast. It was a wonderful cast. The first day, when we introduced Ophelia to Kate Burton, Kate promptly said, "I'm sorry, I can't hold the cat. I'm allergic to cats." At which point Eva Le Gallienne and our production stage manager turned to me and said, "Bill, what are you going to do about this?" I thought it was the oddest question I had ever heard. If someone's allergic to an animal, there's really nothing you can do to the animal to stop the allergy. I wondered why Kate hadn't said anything before, knowing there was going to be a real cat in the show. But they put the onus on me to make this go away.

I went home that afternoon to the apartment, and we started calling groomers all over New York City, trying to find a way to de-allergize a cat. Most of them thought we were crazy and wouldn't even bathe a cat. The other half said there's no such thing as de-allergizing an animal. On the second day, we started calling groomers in New Jersey and Connecticut because we didn't know what else to do. I ran across a man in Fort Lee, New Jersey, who had a grooming school. When I told him the situation, he said, "No problem. Bring the cat in and I'll take care of her." We ran over to New Jersey, I waited, and two hours later, he handed Ophelia back to me. She looked a little cleaner but otherwise the same. He said, "That should work." I ran her to rehearsal and told them the cat was de-allergized. Kate said, "This is great. I'm not sneezing." We did the scene and everything was fine. (I later learned that the miracle treatment was Downy fabric softener, believe it or not. I don't know why it worked, but it did, and we brought Ophelia in for her treatment once a week for the rest of the run.)

Our first preview with an audience was December 8. Both animals performed brilliantly and continued to perform until December 23, which was our opening night. During that time we had also gotten some sad news—*Annie* was going to be closing in January 1983. Still, this meant that for the last two weeks of December, we would have two shows running on Broadway again, which made us very proud. But we were also looking at the end of an era.

We were now housing Hamletta and Ophelia in our apartment across the street, walking them over to the theater and then walking them home at night. We told our doorman, who knew Sandy and also knew where we worked, that we had two cats in the show. We had gotten two little covered carriers, one for the pig and one for the cat. The doorman was always interested in saying hello to the animals, but we couldn't let him, primarily because we didn't want him (or the landlord) to know we were keeping a pig in the apartment. Well, as Hamletta got used to getting into the crate, she would snort. The first time we were walking by the doorman and she snorted, he said, "What was that?"

Of course, I said, "Well, it was the cat."

"She sounds sick," he said.

"Yeah, she's got a cold, she doesn't feel good," I said, and we hurried off. The doorman was very concerned that our cat had a lingering cold and would ask about her every day.

Meanwhile, members of the press department were working overtime getting publicity for the show. In her column, Liz Smith mentioned how two Broadway stars were sleeping together—the pig from *Alice in Wonderland* and Sandy from *Annie*.

My parents and my best friend, Dave, and his new wife came into New York to attend the opening. We were at the apartment and I was showing Dave this little pig that lived in a refrigerator box in my office. Dave said he would like to feed her. We were laughing at how crazy my life had become, and I forgot to tell Dave to hold the bottle level so the milk didn't run into her lungs. All of a sudden Hamletta started to choke. She was having trouble catching her breath. Dave looked at me, panicked, and said, "What do we do?"

"I don't know," I said. "The milk must have gotten into her lungs."

"How can we get it out?" Dave said.

"Pick her up by her back legs and hold her upside down?" I yelled.

Dave did just that, but touching her made Hamletta panic, and she tried to squeal. My mother in the other room called out, "What's going on in there?"

I yelled back, "The pig is choking, and we're trying to save her!"

My father had grown up on a farm in the mountains of Italy. He came into the room and saw Dave holding the pig upside down while I tried to compress her chest to push the milk out and the pig gasped for air. In his broken accent he started yelling at us, demanding to know what we were doing to that poor pig.

"Pop, we got to save her!" I said. By now she was getting limp. My father yelled again, telling us to leave the poor thing alone because we were only making it worse. By now she was silent. Dad came over and took her from us and put her down on the floor. Dave and I were in shock—we thought we killed her. Dad just knelt over her and a few seconds later she burped and tried to get up and run. "What are you, crazy?" Dad said.

Hamletta was still coughing, so we called the Animal Medical Center and ran her over to be examined. They gave her antibiotics to prevent any upper respiratory infection, and the exotic animal doctor reminded me to make sure her bottles were level. He added that if it happened again, just let her cough it out. We didn't tell the doctor we had tried to do pig CPR.

Opening night came; the reviews were mixed. It was a show meant for family audiences and kids. It got good reviews for its classic nature, but it really wasn't high-tech enough for most young audiences of the day. Things were rough—it didn't look like the show was going to run for very long. Also, opening before Christmas meant a lot of people bought tickets for presents. Going into January, it's harder to sell tickets because everyone is paying holiday bills. It was a tough time to be trying to run a show that didn't get rave reviews.

By the time we opened, Hamletta was almost six weeks old and about 30 pounds. She was getting too heavy for Kate Burton to carry. We had known this was coming, and a week before we opened, we had gotten another baby pig and started training her with the baby bottle and the jingle bells, to have her ready to replace Hamletta. A week after we had opened, when things had calmed down, we replaced the pig and even that news made the New York *Daily News* and other news outlets around the country.

Annie closed on January 2, 1983. *Alice in Wonderland* closed a week later. It was a very solemn time in our year—what I believed was the end of my career, even though I now had four Broadway shows to my credit. We had succeeded in both plays and musicals; trained dogs, cats, and pigs; and had helped a lot of shelter animals along the way.

One interesting side note: Later that year, PBS decided to film the version of *Alice in Wonderland* with Kate. We were to work with some of the greats of the theater we had worked with previously. In this version, Kate was reunited with her father, Richard Burton, who played the White Knight. Also in the cast were Eve Arden, Kaye Ballard, Geoffrey Holder, Nathan Lane, Donald O'Connor, and Austin Pendleton, as well as many other talented cast members. So we got a chance to re-create our roles, both with Ophelia and another new pig from the 4-H Club of Hunterdon County, and also to see Mr. Burton perform with his daughter once again.

Alice in Wonderland turned out to be one of those pivotal times in my life. It showed the power of publicity and how it could help a show—but it also showed that I was able to create press events that would become beneficial for selling tickets and raising animal awareness. At the end of the run, the pigs went back to their farms where they lived long, healthy lives, and Ophelia was adopted by one of the dressers in the show. He was an older gentleman who was by himself. He had just lost his cat, and he had always come down to visit her. We decided she would be better off living one-on-one with a person who had no other animals and a very quiet lifestyle, instead of living in a house with eight dogs and other animals. She lived another fifteen years with this gentleman before she passed away.

Chapter 7

Cameron Mackintosh vs. the Bull Terriers

In the fall of 1983, I was contacted by the general managers of *Annie*, who were representing Cameron Mackintosh, the young British producer of *Cats*. For his next production, he had done a very successful revival of *Oliver* in London. *Oliver* was his favorite musical, and it was his vision to bring it back to Broadway. He wanted the revival to be very close to the original production, and had even hired the original director and one of the stars. The call for this show couldn't have come at a better time. *Annie* and *Alice in Wonderland* had closed in January. I had spent most of that year setting up productions of *Annie* all around the country and doing guest appearances with Sandy. So even though this was a revival, I was very excited.

Oliver is a musical version of *Oliver Twist*. The villain, Bill Sikes, has a dog named Bull's-Eye that appears in several scenes. At the climax of the story, the dog leads an angry mob to find Sikes after he has murdered his girlfriend. We found out that a bull terrier played Bull's-Eye in the original production. You've probably seen bull terriers—the Target store chain uses one as a mascot—but they're a fairly rare breed. They're pretty odd looking, with a long Roman nose, triangular eyes, and pointed ears; white bull terriers, like the one in the play, look a little like pigs. They were originally bred to fight, so they are powerful dogs, very determined, and they can be very aggressive

Graeme Campbell, as Bill Sikes, with Buffy in the revival of *Oliver*.
Photo by Martha Swope, © New York Public Library for the Performing Arts

toward other animals. But they adore humans—the people who bred them to fight also bred them to love people, so they wouldn't bite their handlers.

Because they're a rare breed, I had a difficult time finding good dogs. Besides doing my shelter search, I also contacted breeders throughout the country. I found a respected breeder who agreed to lend us an eight-year-old female named Buffy, who got along well with other dogs, in return for publicity and a fee.

In the play, the first time Bull's-Eye enters the stage he's being carried, and the second time he's walking on a leash and has to stay calm while Bill Sikes gets very violent. In the final scene, the dog has to run through a crowd of angry townspeople and lead them to Sikes. I decided I needed two dogs: one that was trained to do the final scene and a calmer dog to do the quiet scenes. I found the second dog at the Westchester Humane Society. Lydia had been brought in for medical treatment after being abandoned. In addition to recovering from surgery, she was at least ten—old for a bull terrier. So she was quiet and calm, fine for the early scenes, but she could never do the final scene. I still needed one more dog as an understudy.

Then I got a call from the American Society for the Prevention of Cruelty to Animals in Manhattan. The FBI had broken up a dog-fighting ring, and one of the dogs was a beautiful male bull terrier. He didn't get along with other dogs, but he was very good with humans. His name was Vito. When I went to see this dog, I found he *was* a magnificent specimen of a bull terrier—big, strong, handsome—but what struck me was the way he'd very calmly look in your eyes and follow your every move. I didn't really think I could use him in the show because of his fighting background, but there was something about his attentiveness that I really liked, so I decided to adopt him. So, by December I had the three bull terriers: Buffy would be trained for the final scene, Lydia would be the dog that was in the quiet scenes, and Vito—on paper, at least—would be the backup for both those dogs.

I soon found out that Vito had heartworms, which can be fatal to dogs. The treatment is almost as bad as the disease—my vet had treated O'Malley, who had been in *Annie* on Broadway, for it. The recovery time can be quite long. When he returned after being freed of the heartworms, we had to be very careful because he was so aggressive with other animals. But he was very sweet with humans—he loved to be petted and have his belly rubbed, and he looked into your eyes with so much gratitude when you were kind to him. Vito seemed to be completely untrained, which I thought was probably because he had been a fighting dog. You could call him and he would never come—he wouldn't even turn to look at you. I let it slide because he'd so far had such a horrible, brutal life, and he was finally on the road to recovery. I never thought he would have to be in the show, he was an understudy on paper only, so I let him enjoy being outside in the sun.

Then one day a kid set off a firecracker in the next yard. All the dogs in the house started barking—except for Vito, who was looking blissfully in another direction. I became suspicious, so I walked up slowly behind him, yelling his name and clapping my hands. He didn't move. I was right behind him and he didn't turn around. Then I tapped him on the shoulder, and he turned and acted very happy to see me. I realized that he wasn't untrained, he was completely deaf. That was the reason he was so attentive. If he wasn't looking at you, he didn't know that you were speaking to him. I found out from breed experts that deafness is one of the possible hereditary problems with bull terriers. I was heartbroken because I loved this dog so much. I thought there would really be no way for me to train a deaf dog in a theatrical situation. If the show became a hit, I would have to find another understudy and help find Vito a good home.

Rehearsals for *Oliver* started in March, and we began getting the cast used to the dogs. We also had to get the dogs accustomed to wearing makeup—we had to paint a black bull's-eye around one eye. I didn't bring Vito with me because at that point, I didn't think it would be important for him to get to know anyone. Because he was so difficult to handle when he was around the other dogs, he just stayed at home and rested. Lydia and Buffy came in every day to socialize with the cast, and then I would have a session with the actor who played Sikes. He would carry them around, and we also worked on getting them to walk by his side and stay. We couldn't really do the final scene until we got into the theater. They showed me a model of the set, and explained that Buffy would have to run up a staircase, across a bridge that was sixteen feet off the ground, and then come down another staircase and out a door, with the cast running and screaming behind her.

Believe it or not, I didn't think that it would be too hard. As long as the dog knew the pattern and was sure of getting a treat at the end, it should be a piece of cake. The key was that Buffy would have to learn everything on the set, so she could get used to the actual stairs, bridge, and the noise. That made me a little nervous, because we wouldn't have a chance to do that until a week before the show opened.

Then I was thrown another curve. Sam Stickler was the stage manager for this show, and he had also worked as a stage manager on the national tours of *Annie*. He and I had very different ideas about how we should rehearse the dogs and how the dogs should behave. On a few occasions on *Annie* I had to ask Martin Charnin, the director, to decide how we should do things, and Martin told Sam to do whatever I wanted. It was pretty embarrassing for a stage manager to be told he had to listen to a dog trainer. Well, Sam apparently chose this show for payback. And he did it in such a way—by giving the appearance of trying to accommodate me or by claiming a situation was out of his control—that he made it seem like *he* wasn't doing anything wrong.

I had explained to Sam that I would need a minimum of one hour alone onstage with Buffy, to teach her the pattern. But rehearsal time is expensive. On a Broadway production, everyone belongs to a union. There are unions for the actors, directors, lighting designers, choreographers, stagehands—even the ushers—everyone except dogs and dog trainers. These unions have very strict rules about what can be done onstage and when it can be done. For example, the stagehands' union requires that every time there's a rehearsal onstage, anywhere from four to eight stagehands have to be paid a four-hour minimum, even if they don't move a single piece of scenery. If you want to work onstage during a lunch hour or dinner break, for the crew, that's overtime. So when we get to the theater, the priority is always to get the actors ready without wasting crew time. I have to rely on the production stage manager to talk to the director, the actors, and the stagehands to help find time to rehearse the dogs.

The first day we were in the theater, I was told there was no time available, which was fine. I walked the dogs through the theater, getting them used to the different areas, having them in the wings. Next day, again, there was no time scheduled for me to rehearse the big scene with Buffy. I reminded Sam that it was his job to find me the hour I needed, and he said he would try.

Finally, on the fourth day, we got to the scene and I had the stage. I put Buffy on a leash and led her up the stairs, over the bridge, and down the other side. She was afraid because the bridge was slippery, and we made a note to put carpet down. When I tried to take her across again, the director said we had to move on. When I said I needed more time, he told me to talk to Sam. When I found Sam later, he said he was just following the schedule the director had set out, and it was my problem. He simply wasn't going to help me at all. Fortunately, bull terriers are smart. Even though she had only been on the stage a couple of times, Buffy came out and did her part in the final technical and dress rehearsals. But she was very tentative, and it was clear to me that she was frightened—and it was getting worse.

Our first preview was on a Thursday night, and I had no idea what would happen. The first part of the show went very well. When Buffy walked onto the stage for the final scene, the audience made a very audible cheer, at which point she turned around, ran offstage, and went straight to the dressing room. One of the actors covered by ad-libbing, "I think Bill Sikes is over there!"—and they all ran off. Back in my dressing room at the end of the show, I felt terrible—not because Buffy didn't do her part, but because she hadn't had enough time in rehearsals to get over her fear.

All of a sudden a young man with dark hair flung open my dressing-room door. In a British accent, he rudely asked why Buffy hadn't done her trick. I turned around and said, "Excuse me, but who are you, and what are you thinking, coming into my dressing room?" It was Cameron Mackintosh, the producer, and he was unhappy with both me and Buffy. I was taken aback because I had never met Cameron Mackintosh before. I had

"Aren't they cute?"
Photo by Clarence Davis/New York Daily News

seen him, but he had never introduced himself to me. Also, I thought he was being extremely unprofessional, and he was upsetting the dogs. That made me angry, so I stood up to him in a way I might not have otherwise. I told him, "The dog's not performing because we haven't been provided the proper rehearsal." Cameron said we'd have the stage at 12:30 P.M. the next day, but he expected to see a perfect performance that night. Then he stormed out.

We were there the next day at noon. Rehearsal was due to start at 1:00, but the theater was locked, leaving us standing in the street. I argued with the doorman, pointing out that Cameron Mackintosh had arranged the time for us, but the doorman refused to unlock the door. Sam came nearly an hour later. When I confronted him, he claimed that he had forgotten we were supposed to have the stage. By then it was too late—rehearsal was starting. That night, like the night before, Buffy went out, heard the audience, turned around, and ran back offstage. And like the night before, Cameron Mackintosh came storming into my room without knocking, saying, "I told you I was going to fire you if the dog didn't perform, and she didn't perform!"

I said, "Excuse me. I didn't get rehearsal today." When he insisted he had left orders for us to get rehearsal, I told him to check with the stage manager. "The time was not arranged," I told him. At that point he said we'd have time the next day, but he wanted to see Buffy perform at the matinee. We did get the stage for a half-hour before the show. Unfortunately, by that time, almost all of Buffy's time onstage had been frightening for her.

She was very tentative about going onstage and climbing those stairs—in fact, she was shaking when she did it during rehearsal. I thought we might have to do this every day—to reassure her before every show—but when I asked Sam if we could do that, he only said, "We'll see."

That afternoon, for the third show in a row, Buffy went out, heard the audience, and ran off the stage. Mr. Mackintosh, for the third time in a row, came to see me after the show and wanted to know what was going wrong. Again I tried to explain about the lack of rehearsal, but he said he didn't care. I had one more chance to get Buffy to do the trick, or I was fired. It probably was one of the lowest moments in my life. I had been painted into a corner, and there was no way I could get myself out of it. I thought my career as a trainer would be ruined. We had the stage set aside from six to seven o'clock. I knew that Buffy had been scared past the point of no return and that no amount of rehearsal time could help now. Lydia couldn't do it—she was so arthritic she had to be carried upstairs.

There was only one dog left.

Up until this point, Vito had been living the good life. He had two meals a day. Even though we had to keep him separate from the other dogs, he had people who cared for him and he had a comfy bed. Because noise didn't wake him up, he spent a lot of time sleeping. I had taught him basic obedience—*sit* and *stay*—using the same hand signals I used with the other dogs, and as long as he was looking at me, he was a quick learner. I even had a special way of exercising him. Because he couldn't hear me when I called him, I couldn't let him run free without a leash. He loved to fetch, but he didn't always see where the ball went, so you could throw it only a few feet. Then one night when I took him for a walk, I brought a flashlight with me. He started to chase the spot of light on the ground like it was a ball. I was amazed. I put him on his tether and let him chase the light for about twenty minutes until he just dropped with happy exhaustion. I was pleased we had found a game he could play.

We had started bringing Vito to the theater and keeping him in his crate in the dressing room so that we could walk him and care for him during the long days of rehearsals and performances. Vito was the only dog I had that was a bull terrier and, unlike Lydia, could at least walk upstairs, but I had not done any work with him. All I had done was make him healthy and exercise him with a flashlight. Dejected over the situation with Buffy, I brought Vito down to the stage and sat with him. He stayed beside me, watching my every move. I couldn't think of any way to train him for the play. He couldn't hear the commands, and he wouldn't be able to see me if he wasn't looking in the right direction when I gave the cue. Just to give him some exercise, I pulled the flashlight out and started shining it on the stage. He was really focused on it—he thought we had a new indoor play space. He was so intent that when I ran the beam up the steps he followed it, and then he followed it back down.

I couldn't believe what I was seeing. I asked my assistant to hold him stage right. I climbed the stairs to the bridge, then flashed the light through the pattern. Vito chased it up the stairs, across the bridge, and down the other side. I turned off the flashlight and gave him a biscuit. We brought him back stage right and I showed him the pattern again, this time shielding the light so it wasn't as bright. He did it perfectly. He couldn't wait to get his biscuit on the other side. Then we tried it the way it would happen in the show. I stood in the wings stage left, my assistant held Vito stage right. On cue, I turned on the light and he ran up the stairs, across the bridge, down the other side, and over to me to get his cookie. We did it six times in all, and he did it perfectly every time. I was stunned. At this point we had spent almost two and a half months training Buffy, and all that training had been wasted because she was so frightened of the stage. Here was a dog that had lived through brutal fights, had survived a deadly disease, was deaf, and was thankful just to play with me and a flashlight and get a cookie, yet he had done the behavior perfectly six times in a row. At that moment, I thought there might be a chance.

That night, we did the first two scenes in the first act as usual. As the big scene approached, I showed Vito the flashlight. I ran around to the other side of the stage and shined it up the staircase. To my amazement he ran up the steps, over the bridge, and down the other side with the cast chasing behind him, screaming, "Where's Bill Sikes?" and the audience cheering. It was a miracle. Of course, when I stopped to think about it, I realized he didn't need to get used to the noise and commotion in the theater. He couldn't hear it. And because we had done the behavior just two hours earlier, he recognized it immediately. As far as he was concerned, we were just playing the same game we had played in the empty theater.

Cameron Mackintosh never came back to say congratulations, and Sam Stickler never said a word. Neither did the director. But the cast and the crew were ecstatic. They called him St. Vito for creating a miracle. That odd-looking, deaf dog had saved my career. Unfortunately, the show got mixed to bad reviews. The director had re-created his original production, but Broadway had changed a lot in twenty years, and the show now seemed dated. *Oliver* closed after thirteen previews and seventeen performances. That put me in a tough situation. I had really come to love these crazy bull terriers, and I wanted to keep them. But bull terriers demand a lot from their owners, a real commitment of time and energy, and I couldn't give that to them. I had to do what was right for the dogs and find them homes. Buffy, of course, was easy. She returned to her owner, who was very glad to have her back. Lydia was adopted by a cast member, and she spent the rest of her life on a nice, comfy couch.

I thought Vito, with his deafness and his aggression, would be difficult to place. But after the miracle of being rescued from fighting and the miracle in the theater, St. Vito had one more miracle coming. We found a wonderful breeder who took in only dogs that had been fought brutally and let them live the rest of their lives in peace. And there, Vito got all the love and attention he deserved.

Chapter 8

Anything Goes at Lincoln Center

In the mid-1980s, Broadway was reeling from "the British Invasion." Most of the big hits were musical extravaganzas like *Cats* and *Phantom of the Opera*. Few shows were being produced with roles for animals. After *Annie* closed in 1983, I worked on a series of *Annie* revivals, off-Broadway shows, regional theater, television, and films. But by 1986 I was thirty years old and disillusioned with the entertainment field. I had garnered a lot of respect as an animal trainer for Broadway, but at this point, mostly to pay the rent, I had to work at just about anything.

I really disliked the film work. Animals—and animal trainers—were very much an afterthought in films. Check the credits the next time you watch a movie. If an animal is involved, even in a major role, the credit is placed near the bottom of the list, somewhere after the caterers. Animals were treated like props, and we were usually hired by the props department. There never was a chance to talk with the writer, director, actors, or creative team until the day of the shoot, so it was hard to prepare the animals for what they really needed to do. We were often given incorrect information, and things were constantly changing. Rehearsal on the set was nonexistent, and the pressure was very high because you have to get

The cast of *Anything Goes* at Lincoln Center. *Photo by Photofest/Brigette Lacombe*

the whole project done in a certain amount of time that was entirely based on the budget.

In addition, now I had become just one of many that provided animals for the entertainment field in New York City. But with no unions for animal trainers, the producers made us bid against each other to keep rates down. The agencies were very competitive, and when I tried to organize a union, the response was, "Go ahead. We won't join. We'll underbid you and get all the work." So I made the decision to get out of animal training altogether and move back to Connecticut. The only thing I really knew how to do was theater, so I hoped to get into producing or theater management. I found a small house in Haddam—a two-bedroom prefab on four acres—close to the Goodspeed Opera House, where my career had started. In the fall of 1986, I loaded up the truck and moved to what I called "the farm" with my ten dogs, three cats, and two goats.

After looking for a while, I decided to take a job at Goodspeed as house manager. I still had many friends there. Sandy was twelve years old and a local hero, so I went back. It wasn't really the job I wanted, but at least I was working back in the theater with a weekly paycheck. Then, in the summer of 1987, soon after I had started my job at Goodspeed, New York's Lincoln Center decided to do a revival of the Cole Porter musical, *Anything Goes*. Lincoln Center called the Goodspeed, looking for "that guy" who trained the dog for *Annie*. Just as I was moving out of Broadway and New York, Broadway was calling me back.

Except it wasn't really Broadway. Lincoln Center is a major cultural institution that does absolutely first-class productions. They present all types of performances—music, dance, theater, opera—drawing a wide variety of audiences. But because Lincoln Center is a nonprofit organization, it is considered an off-Broadway theater. And while it's a great credit to have, actors and stagehands at Lincoln Center get paid about half the salary of their Broadway counterparts. Lincoln Center, at the time, was paying their actors $650 for a minimum core salary. They would only pay $400 for a trainer and two dogs to be used in *Anything Goes*. I was really torn about this production. The pay wasn't great, but I was drawn to it because of the talent involved. Patti Lupone was starring, and Jerry Zaks was making his directorial debut. But after years of struggling and the decision to walk away, I wasn't sure I wanted to go back to New York. Outside of *Oliver,* I hadn't had a Broadway show in five years. At around the same time, Goodspeed was preparing a new musical based on the old Little Rascals/ Our Gang comedies. They needed an American Staffordshire terrier, generally known as a pit bull, to play Pete the Pup. As far as Goodspeed was concerned, they had a built-in trainer on staff once again, which was me. With *Little Rascals* opening, and the chance of another hit like *Annie* here in Connecticut, I decided to return to training.

I told Lincoln Center that the money wasn't enough to acquire dogs, set up housing, and cover transportation back and forth to the theater. I suggested finding someone who already lived near the theater, who had two dogs, and who could work cheaply. I would train them and supervise them for the show. That solution seemed agreeable to everyone, so we put a notice in the theatrical newspaper *Backstage.* A lot of unemployed actors responded, and we hired an older actress and her two untrained Yorkies who lived near the theater. Goodspeed agreed to help me make time to get to rehearsals in New York to set up *Anything Goes*, come back to East Haddam to set up rehearsals for *Little Rascals*, and then also run the theater at night.

Because *Anything Goes* was a revival of an older musical, the dog was really just used as a sight gag. In the plot, a young socialite and her mother, who owns the little dog, go on a very fancy cruise in search of a rich husband. But the young socialite has fallen in love with a poor musician who stows away on the boat to be with her. He finds the small dog and shaves off its fur to make a false beard for himself as a disguise. In the final scene, when everyone is reconciled, the captain brings out a hairless dog and asks if it belongs to anyone. The dog is returned to the mother and everyone lives happily ever after.

The director wanted the dog to make entrances to the center of the stage, but because Lincoln Center was trying to do a first-class production on a low budget, they decided to pay for just one week of rehearsal. While the two Yorkies were very sweet, they were also very spoiled and untrained. That meant the best we could do was have them carried around onstage. Getting the dogs set up, instructing the actress on how to handle them backstage, and running the show was very simple: One of the dogs was used with a long coat, and the other dog was shaved so that she had very short hair. Everything seemed to be fine. *Anything Goes* was a very smart, witty production with the music of Cole Porter. It got rave reviews and became an overnight hit. The show would ultimately run almost two years.

The opening-night party at Lincoln Center was very exciting. It felt very good to be back in a hit again. The dogs were getting mentioned in some of the reviews, reestablishing my name in New York. Then I immediately turned around and went back to Goodspeed to open *Little Rascals*, where Pete the Pup had a fairly large role. Unfortunately, the reviews for that show weren't as good. The creative team kept working, trying to create another family-friendly musical like *Annie*. Unfortunately, the composer, Joe Raposo, became ill and the show never really came together. It closed after the scheduled run.

As *Anything Goes* settled in for its run, the actress we had hired to handle the dogs started to let the success of the show go to her head. She wanted more money, and she started demanding better treatment backstage. I was getting calls from the stage managers and company managers, asking if I could please talk to her and straighten her out. As much as I tried, she felt that because her little dogs were the canine stars of the show, she deserved more, even though she had a signed contract. It became clear by November that we would have to ask her to leave.

Then I was faced with the problem of having to fulfill my contract on the budget provided. One of my trainers, Lane Haverly, agreed that he would move back to New York and do the show. Once he rented an apartment, he would be working for almost nothing, but he would do it just to preserve our careers. The plan was for him to take over around Christmas, which meant we only had a month to find two new dogs. I started searching area pounds for small Yorkies that were calm, sweet, and nonaggressive. I wasn't having any luck finding two dogs, so I was forced to call reputable breeders in the area.

We finally found a dog at a breeder in Oxford, Connecticut. She had several litters of teacup Yorkies that were much larger than the breed standard, so they couldn't be sold as teacups. The breeder just wanted to get rid of them, so we adopted a young male named Oscar, who had the right temperament to be in the show, to be the main dog. As we were looking for the dog that would be shaved, we heard of another breeder who had an older dog they were going to euthanize because she wasn't producing puppies anymore. The dog's name was Windy.

When we saw Windy, she looked twice her age. When breeders have dogs produce litter after litter without a break, the mothers start losing calcium because they're producing milk for the puppies, and their overall health suffers. Their bones get brittle and their teeth fall out. When we found Windy she was six or seven years old, but she walked like she had arthritis, she had hair loss over the majority of her body, and she had no teeth. When dogs don't have any teeth in their mouths, there's nothing to keep their tongue in, so it just sort of hangs out to the side. She actually looked very comical, like she had been beat up and was a little knocked out. We felt so sorry for this dog that we adopted her as the second dog. There was no budget for an understudy, so we had to make sure neither of these dogs got sick.

Once we had Oscar and Windy, we moved Lane Haverly into my old apartment on West 52nd Street, and then he took over. We got the show back on track and everything seemed to be going well. In the summer of 1988, Lincoln Center decided that they were going to send out a national

Oscar is De-Lovely.
Photo by Lane Haverly

tour, setting it up as a commercial venture—a nationwide, for-profit tour starring Leslie Uggams, Rex Smith, and Rip Taylor. We started rehearsal for that production in September. Instead of using Yorkies, the director decided to use a Pomeranian and a Chihuahua so that in the first scene, it was a very furry, fuzzy dog, and in the end it was completely bald. This was another case where I felt we'd get the best results if the dogs were being handled by someone with a very similar background to mine. All my trainers were busy, so I asked my cousin Rhona Hanson if she would go out with the tour, and she did.

The tour went out in October 1988 and didn't do as well as they had hoped. The dogs were retired by the spring, but the director liked the look of the Chihuahua as the shaved dog, and brought her into the New York production for a while. Ultimately they decided to put Windy back in, and she and Oscar stayed with the show until it closed in September 1989, after 784 performances.

The dogs were very loved by the company. They had their own small dressing room, but every night Oscar would sneak out to say hello to the rest of the cast. When the show closed, Lane Haverly adopted him, and they had a good life together. Windy was so debilitated when we first got her that she could only walk a few feet before becoming exhausted. We brought her to a holistic vet who gave us nutritional advice and set up a healthy diet for her. When a dog is that old and is having health problems, I generally don't put her up for adoption. It isn't fair to the new owners, who will have to assume all the extra work and medical expenses that come with an older dog—and it isn't fair to the dog. So Windy came back to the farm and lived with me for another three years until she finally passed away.

Chapter 9

Sandy Gets Bad Reviews

Right before Christmas of 1988, I got a call from the general managers of the original production of *Annie*. They invited me to the apartment of Charles Strouse, our composer, for a private reading. They wouldn't tell me anything more, saying only that it was "very secret." When I arrived at Charles's penthouse, it was like old home week. Martin Charnin was there, along with Tom Meehan, who wrote the book. Dorothy Loudon, who had won the Tony Award for playing Miss Hannigan on Broadway, was also there, along with many of the original management team and a number of other potential investors. After a few drinks we all sat down in front of a piano. I was about to witness my first backers' audition.

When they started, they said they'd be presenting their idea for the sequel to *Annie*, called *Annie 2: Miss Hannigan's Revenge*. Martin and Tom had talked about writing a sequel, and this was it. They explained they were putting together a proposed multimillion-dollar extravaganza. Then they began narrating it and singing some of the songs. It was a spoof of the original production, not at all what we had expected. The role of Miss Hannigan was greatly expanded. The plot was that she breaks out of jail, kidnaps Annie, and substitutes a double, then plans to marry Daddy Warbucks, kill him and the real Annie, and steal his money. To those of us who had worked

Kathyn Zaremba, as Annie, with Cindy Lou in *Annie Warbucks*. *Photo by Carol Rosegg*

on the original show, it was hilarious—funny, clever, full of twists. Sandy's part was also expanded. He discovers Miss Hannigan's plot, tries to expose it, then identifies the real Annie in the last act to save the day.

The mood at the end of this reading was joyous. Two months later I had a copy of the script. The original Sandy was too old now to do this show, but I had been working with a dog named Beau, adopted from the American Society for the Prevention of Cruelty to Animals in New York. He had been doing regional productions of *Annie* and had a real stage presence. The original Sandy had floppy ears, but Beau had pointy ears, just like the Sandy in the comic strip. I thought he would work. When Martin met him, he loved him, and we had our Sandy for *Annie 2*.

They did a nationwide search for the new Annie, selecting a young actress named Danielle Findley. Over the coming months, she worked very hard with Beau. We began rehearsals in New York in September 1989 and traveled to Washington, D.C., for previews and performances in December. The official Broadway opening was scheduled for March 1990. Before we even left for Washington, the marquee was up in New York, a big ANNIE 2 on the Marriott Marquis Theater. Because of my long-standing relationship with the creators and producers, I got title-page credit in the program for the first time. It took me out of the league of just being part of the crew and elevated me to the same level as a designer or creator.

We had only one problem with the training: At the climax of the play, when Miss Hannigan is about to marry Daddy Warbucks, Martin wanted Beau to erupt into barking when the minister asks if anyone objects to the wedding and says, "Speak now or forever hold your peace." Beau did bark on cue, but it was not the excited outburst that Martin wanted. One week before previews started, I was still stumped about how to make this happen. Then, driving home one night, as we passed Central Park, Beau went crazy when he saw the horses waiting to take people on carriage rides. That was it. I convinced one of our production assistants, Jeff Markowitz, to wear a horse costume during rehearsal one day. On cue, we let Beau get a glimpse, and he went nuts—Martin almost fell off his chair laughing, but it was just what he wanted. Poor Jeff had to put on that horse costume for every performance during our Washington run.

The first preview of *Annie 2* at the Kennedy Center was sold out. We were all excited to see the audience reaction. Then something strange happened. The audience didn't like it. We had forgotten that the original *Annie* had only become a hit when they made Annie a real character the audience could root for. Adults in the audience who had grown up loving *that* Annie were upset we had turned her back into a comic strip character. The kids they brought with them to the theater were actually frightened by several scenes—we saw them crying and leaving the theater before the end of the first act.

The next forty-eight hours were a blur. The reviews were horrible. The *Washington Post* even gave Beau a bad review for not looking like the original Sandy. It was a multimillion-dollar mistake. I remember going to visit Martin in his room at the Watergate Hotel. I just wanted to give him a hug and make sure he was okay, but he was already talking about how we could rewrite the show. The New York opening was canceled, and by the end of our run in Washington, there were the beginnings of a whole new musical.

Two months later I got a call from Martin. The Goodspeed Opera House had agreed to do a new version of *Annie 2* in their small space, the Norma Terris Theatre, starting in May. The one thing that Martin wanted me to do was find a new dog that looked exactly like our original Sandy. I rallied all my contacts, and my friends at The Associated Humane Society in Newark came through again. In March I adopted Chelsea, who was only about eight months old, very hyper, but she could have been Sandy's twin. Chelsea was probably given up at the shelter because she was young and wild and undisciplined. All the time as we were trying to get her used to being onstage, we had to train her in all the basics.

Martin, Tom, and Charles had done a tremendous amount of rewriting, and what was once a spoof had now become the tale of a single father trying to find a mother for his child. The show would run for ten weeks, with the hope that it would be transferred to New York. Most of the cast was new, including our Annie—Lauren Gaffney, who is still a good friend of mine. So I was starting from scratch with a new kid, a new dog, and a very short rehearsal period. While Chelsea tried, she was very nervous on stage. Lauren worked very hard to get her through, but any little sound and Chelsea spooked. She had the look, but at this point she didn't have the presence I like in a stage dog. Between these struggles, Norma Terris's death, and Sandy's slowing down with age, it was bittersweet being back at Goodspeed, in a theater named for my old benefactor, working on another show.

In ten weeks they were able to refine the play into a family musical that a lot of people enjoyed, and the reviews were certainly much better than in Washington. When we closed at Goodspeed in July, we were told that a new tour would be mounted very soon, and hopefully we would be going back to Broadway. In August, I headed down to North Carolina for a production of *Annie*. By then our original Sandy was slowing down. He was still very vital, but he had paralysis and weakness in his back legs from arthritis. He couldn't really walk, so I had to carry him outside when he needed to relieve himself, just as I did when his hip was dislocated so many years ago. He still came with me to the theater every day because he hated to be left alone. I would carry him in and he would rest on his pillow in the dressing room until the end of the show, and then come home with me.

Beau was going to be doing the North Carolina show, but I took Sandy with me because he needed constant care. It was a two-day trip going down, and Sandy did very well. I had customized my car so that he could be lying right next to me in the front seat, while Beau had the backseat with all our belongings. On the second day of rehearsal, Sandy became very ill. He had to be hospitalized, and we didn't think he was going to make it through the night. A wonderful local vet stabilized him; Sandy rallied and was happy to see me the next day when I went to pick him up. But the doctor told me he didn't know how much longer Sandy would last because his kidneys weren't functioning at the correct level. He put Sandy on a special diet of easy-to-digest food, and I spent the entire two weeks in North Carolina worrying about his welfare. Every night I would carry him to the theater and he would lie in the dressing room and hear the music. I could tell he wanted to get up and do the show, but he would just wait patiently for me to come back into the room.

After our run, I drove the two days back to Connecticut. The trip had taken a lot out of Sandy—he grew weaker each day. On the morning of Wednesday, August 29, this wonderful dog who had taught me so much, my best friend and companion for nearly half my life, went to sleep and didn't wake up. I cried and I cried and I cried. I called my parents, who had been so good about helping me take care of him. I called Martin Charnin. Then my parents and I took Sandy to be cremated. By the time I got home, there were dozens of messages on my answering machine. Martin had heard in my voice how upset I was and called the folks at Goodspeed, and now everyone was checking to see if I was okay. I didn't answer any of the messages then—I just wanted to be alone so that I could grieve for my old friend.

The next day, the *New York Times* ran an obituary for Sandy. It wasn't a funny piece; it was a serious article about this remarkable dog, highlighting all the wonderful things he had done for audiences, for animals, for children's hospitals, and for charities. It became an international story, and soon I was getting condolences and telegrams and messages from people all around the world. The day after that, August 31, we were scheduled to do an appearance in New York City for *Annie 2*. Martin Charnin had arranged for Lauren Gaffney to sing *I Always Knew*, which they hoped would be the hit song from the show, on a stage at the base of the World Trade Center. Chelsea was supposed to appear with her. I spoke with Martin and told him I didn't think I could do it, but he insisted. When I said I didn't think I could drive, he said he'd send a car. He said I needed to be with the people who loved me and Sandy. I couldn't believe he would ask me to do something like this at the moment of my deepest grief, but I hesitantly agreed.

The next morning at eight o'clock, the limousine came to bring us to New York. Now, not only was I sad over the loss of Sandy, I was also concerned that Chelsea wasn't ready for this performance. She was a very high-strung dog. Even in the Norma Terris Theatre, which only had 200 seats, she would get nervous and run offstage. I was sure she'd be frightened by all the commotion in a live, outdoor performance. When I got there I was still numb from grief. People really didn't understand what I was going through, but Martin said to me, "There's somebody here I think you should see." I turned around and there was Andrea McArdle. I hadn't seen her in years, and we just hugged and cried and talked about good old Sandy. It was probably the best gift Martin ever gave me—the chance to talk about this dog as my friend with the kid who was there when it all started.

Some moments stay with you forever—Lauren Gaffney and Chelsea singing at the World Trade Center.

I believe that sometimes we're given signs—if you look for them, they're usually there. When I led Chelsea up to perform that day, I was hoping beyond all hope that she wouldn't be frightened and drag poor Lauren offstage. As Lauren started singing, Chelsea sat perfectly still. I was incredulous. It was almost as if this wasn't the same dog I had worked with a month ago at Goodspeed. She was looking at me and she was calm. As Lauren hit the last note, a white bird flew over the stage. Now, there are many pigeons in New York, and they can be any color. But white birds are rare, and seeing them fly by themselves is even rarer. In that moment, in my heart of hearts, I felt the spirit of Sandy was sending me a gift and helping us along. As soon as Lauren left the stage, Chelsea dragged her over to me, but for those few minutes, when she needed to do her first public performance for the people of New York City to help promote the show, Chelsea was good.

In January of 1991 I was asked to participate in a new backers' audition. The title had been changed from *Annie 2* to *Annie Warbucks*. Other big changes had been made to the characters and the plot. The creators still had $1 million left of their initial budget. They were looking to raise another $3 million for a commercial production that would come back to Broadway. We did three auditions that February, but that was the last I heard from anyone for a while.

By now it had been six months since I had lost Sandy, but something new had happened. For years, I had felt that I was just a kid lucky enough to find an exceptional dog. Even after I had done other shows all around the country, I always felt insecure about my talent as an animal trainer. Now that special dog was gone, but I found that he had left me with knowledge about how to train animals. I realized that I could either let everything Sandy had taught me die with him, or I could continue moving forward with all I had learned from that wonderful dog. In a sense, that was the real start of my career.

In September I was called by the Marriott Lincolnshire Theater in Chicago. They had agreed to produce *Annie Warbucks*. Since they were a small dinner theater, they didn't have the budget to bring out a lot of people from New York, and they couldn't offer me much money. It would be a real stretch for me to afford it, but since the theater was in a Marriott hotel, they offered to put us up there and let us eat in the employees' lounge, as well as pay us a small salary. The run would be from January until April 1992. It would be another shot at seeing how the new show worked in front of an audience, so I agreed to do it.

Beau was retired from *Annie 2*, although he continued touring with *Annie* until he died a few years later. I needed a new dog to be Chelsea's understudy. In August my vet called me. He was in a neighboring town and had been ordered to euthanize a dog by the local animal warden. He called me up from the pound to say he thought I might be able to use this dog. It was nine o'clock at night, and I had a feeling I was being set up. But even though he wouldn't give me a lot of details, he thought this was a good-looking dog.

When I went to see the dog thirty minutes later, the vet literally had the syringe lying on the table. There in the cage sat a stray they had named Cindy, a reddish, curly-haired dog who had floppy ears and a roman nose (a nose that didn't have a bridge to it) and a white cross on her chest. She had been severely abused and was terrified of people and wouldn't let anybody get near her. Cindy was going to be euthanized because the people who had abandoned her as a puppy had left a collar on her. As she grew, the collar became embedded in her neck. It would require surgery to remove it, and the town wasn't willing to pay for it. I looked at my vet because now I *knew* that he had set me up. I couldn't let this dog die. I told him if he could get the collar off, I would try to train her.

If I thought Chelsea was a long shot for learning how to be a trained dog, she was nothing compared to Cindy. Still, if nothing else, I wanted to save her and find her a good home. Once they removed the collar, even while she was still recovering, Cindy showed a very sweet temperament. She got along well with the other dogs, and she was really very attentive—wild, crazy, un-housebroken, and a bad chewer, but desperately wanting to be loved.

In January of 1992, Chelsea, Cindy, and I drove out to the Marriott Lincolnshire in Chicago, where we would live for the next four months. We would rehearse for two weeks and begin previews at the end of January. This theater was unusual in that the production would be in the round, meaning the audience sat on all sides of the stage. There were no real sets—just furniture, props, and costumes. They were short one actor, so Martin asked me if I would step in and be a marine guard in a couple of the scenes.

It was a strange life, living in a hotel room for four months. Lauren Gaffney, now twelve, and her parents had the adjoining room, so she could sleep with the dogs every night, and I could look after her when her parents had to be away. The show had taken a different direction, and getting used to a whole new cast, new songs, and training a dog while working in the round proved to be a challenge. Chelsea and Lauren certainly tried their best. By then, Lauren had been working with Chelsea for almost a year and a half and was very good at handling her, but Chelsea would still panic when she looked for me and couldn't find me (because there were no wings for me to be in). There were a couple of scenes where I could be onstage with her, but it really became a very difficult situation. We made the best of it, the show got pretty good reviews, and people became more optimistic.

Even though we ran there for almost four months, the creators wanted to work on the show some more. Because the reviews had been good, we were able to move to the Drury Lane Theatre, also in Chicago, where we ran from late April through mid-July. Word of mouth started to spread, and suddenly, audiences were coming to see this wonderful play. Other producers were now coming as well, and the possibility of it becoming the hit we all hoped for was increasing.

While we were there I had the chance to get to know and really train Cindy, whose name had been changed to Cindy Lou by one of the cast. At first Cindy Lou was a handful. She was bouncy and inquisitive, and on more than one occasion, Lauren Gaffney and I had to sneak chewed-on furniture out of our hotel room in the middle of the night, switching it with furniture in the lobby so we wouldn't get charged for the damage. By July her chewing problems had gone away. At first she was frightened of strangers, but the cast was wonderful with her, and she was soon friendly with everyone in the show. Although the scarred area on her neck remained a little sensitive, she really was becoming a very fun, outgoing dog. And as I started to train her, she proved to be a very quick learner. One of my favorite memories of Cindy Lou took place at the Drury Lane Theatre. While we were onstage rehearsing, I had to tie her in the back row because we didn't have a dressing room where I could leave her. When we looked out over the audience, we would see her peeking her nose up over the seats to watch the action. We also had a chance to do understudy rehearsals. In the first few rehearsals that Cindy Lou was onstage, she was actually more relaxed than Chelsea had been in over two years doing the play.

While we were at the Drury Lane, we learned that there would be a five-city national tour of *Annie Warbucks*. The show would be recast with Equity actors out of New York, and everyone hoped it would lead to a Broadway opening. At this point I made an important decision—I decided Cindy Lou should do the tour. I went to Martin and asked him to watch an understudy rehearsal. I said, "I want to use this dog for the tour." He looked at me and said, "Are you sure she has what it takes? You've been

"Next time, we're getting a stylist."
Photo by Diana Walker/ Found Dogs

working with Chelsea for a year and a half." I said, "Martin, she hasn't gotten any better. She's not happy. I think Cindy Lou would be right." He said, "Okay, kid. I hope you can pull it off."

Cindy Lou was almost flawless in rehearsals. Four months later, come opening night in California, she did a nearly perfect show. I was so pleased that in less than a year, this dog—a stray with a collar embedded in her neck, unsure of humans—had gone from being minutes from death to performing in a huge theater in California. Toward the end of the tour we were contacted by a New York producer named Karen Goodwin, who said she would be setting up a production for Broadway. We were going to open on April 21, the sixteenth anniversary of *Annie*'s opening night, and we would be opening in the same theater

Then, in January 1993, the opening was postponed for four weeks. In February it was postponed indefinitely. It was a huge blow for those of us who had been with the production from the beginning, to get so close to Broadway again without opening. Finally, new investors came forward to produce the show off-Broadway, with the opening set for August. By that point, I had found Chelsea a home in Pennsylvania where she would be much happier. I adopted a new dog named Cosmo to be our understudy. And Lauren Gaffney, now thirteen, had outgrown the role of Annie. She was replaced by one of the other orphans, Kathryn Zaremba. I take pride in saying I first saw Kathryn while I was doing a summer stock production of *Annie*. It's not my place to make casting recommendations, but I told Martin he had to see this girl. He hired her to play an orphan in the tour and now gave her the leading role.

When we finally had our New York opening, the show got good reviews. We were even invited to do a special performance at the White House for President and Mrs. Clinton at a Christmas party for the staff. *Annie Warbucks* was a wonderful show. In many ways, I think it was just as good as the original—maybe better—but because of its long, rocky road and the fact it never played on Broadway, it never got the recognition it deserved.

I also remember it for another milestone—Cindy Lou got to "sing" on cue to the music. Never before and never since has a dog been asked to bark in a musical number. But you won't hear Cindy Lou on the cast album. The album producers wouldn't pay for her to come to the recording session, so that's Martin Charnin barking on the album. Just another example of how crazy this business can be.

Kathryn goes from orphan to Annie.
Photo by Carol Rosegg

Chapter 10

Going Bugsy

In the fall of 1990, I was still reeling from the loss of Sandy, just trying to regroup, get my head together, and focus on what my training career would be like without my best friend. I heard rumors of a new play, *La Bête,* that had an animal in it, but no one had called. I found out that the general managers for *La Bête* were the people I had worked with for many years on *Annie.* The director wanted exotic birds onstage, but they decided they didn't want to spend the money to hire a professional animal trainer just to handle the birds. The company manager, Wendy Orshan, had lined up a friend of hers, an actress named Dorothy Hanrahan—they had been friends for many years, since their days together in dinner theater. Wendy knew that Dorothy had owned birds for years, so she convinced Dorothy to go out and find the birds and train them for this play.

La Bête was scheduled to open in Boston in December 1990, and then come to Broadway in January 1991. When I heard the animals were birds, I wasn't too upset about not getting the job. I had never had a bird, I had no experience with birds, and, quite frankly, I didn't think birds were trainable. In October Dorothy went to a bird store she knew in Stamford, Connecticut, her hometown. She bought two one-month-old cockatoos. They

Dylan Baker, as the Prince, with Cicero in *La Bête*. *Photo by Joan Marcus*

were infants, and at one month old, they were still being hand-fed with eye-droppers. She got two so she'd have an understudy. She named the main bird Cicero, and the second was called "B," or B-Bird, since he was "second best." She started hand-taming them and training them, bringing them into New York City to get them used to travel and to the company. The director wanted the character of the prince to hold one of the birds on his arm for a good part of the second act, so the bird was going to have to be calm and quiet onstage for half an hour or more at a time.

At that point, having Dorothy handle the birds seemed to be working well for everyone. The production was saving money by having an amateur animal handler on the show. As an unemployed actress, Dorothy was happy to have the work. Rehearsals in New York ran till mid-December, and then the company traveled to Boston for their out-of-town tryout. As with any new show, the play needed a lot of work. At some point the director decided the second act had problems, and he felt the solution would be to have a dog come out and do a trick. There have been many times in my career when I've been contacted by a show that was in trouble, when someone had the bright idea that putting an animal onstage would turn it into a hit. In this case, the director wanted another character to hand the prince an old shoe. When the prince throws it across the stage in disgust, a door suddenly opens, a dog comes in, picks up the shoe, brings it back to the prince, and runs off.

Near the end of December I got an apologetic call from the general managers. They had to admit that they had gone with another animal trainer in an effort to save money, but now, at the last minute, they needed a dog. They were still trying to save money, so they wondered if I would train their bird handler and just rent them the dog. I was taken aback on many different levels. On the one hand I was angry that they hadn't come to me first, but on the other hand I was happy they came to me as the only person they thought could fix the problem.

At that time I had a little dog, a schnauzer mix named Bugsy, who had done a few shows for me. She was smart, very well trained, and very attentive. Because the show was already up and running and they needed the dog immediately, Bugsy was the only dog I had that I felt could walk into a production, not be frightened by the audience, and do the behavior that they needed. But I was unsure about training someone I didn't know. When I heard that Dorothy was a friend of the company manager and that her only qualification was that she had owned birds, I wasn't at all sure this person would be able to handle Bugsy.

Even if I could train her to handle the dog, because of my experience with *Anything Goes*, I thought it was a bad idea, but I wanted to help. The lead producer on this show was a gentleman by the name of Stuart Ostrow. He had been producing on Broadway for many years, and, in fact, his daughter had been an apprentice at Goodspeed when I was the house manager there. I called Stuart and he was very happy to hear that I would be working on the play. In an effort to cement our relationship for further productions, I offered him a deal unlike any other contract I had signed. I said to him, "Look, I know this is a stretch. I know both financially and artistically, it may or may not work for you. So, instead of my normal contract, pay me a guaranteed amount through the Boston run. Then once we get back to New York and open on Broadway, if at any point you feel the dog isn't working, you can let me go with one week's notice and that will be that."

Stuart and the general managers were very appreciative that I understood what they were going through and that I was interested in helping the production. So a day later I went up to Boston to have Bugsy audition for the director and to meet the bird handler. I remember arriving at the Wilbur Theater, where the show was running, early in the evening. They had a dressing room set up for me. I met the director onstage, and I was able to show him what Bugsy could do. I was invited to watch the show that night.

My dressing room was up on the fourth floor. As I was walking up the stairs, I saw Wendy with two people. One was the stage manager—she introduced the other as her good friend, Dorothy Hanrahan. I had been expecting to meet some conniving gold digger trying to steal my work. Instead, I saw a beautiful woman with emerald green eyes and a sincere smile who said "It's an honor to meet you" as she shook my hand. I immediately became suspicious. My intuition was telling me this was a good soul, but my experience was telling me not to trust her sweet face. Dorothy offered to help me with my bag and with Bugsy. I think I mumbled something stupid, excused myself, and went up to my room. I wanted to watch the show before I made any decisions.

It was a very interesting show—a modern-day verse play, very dramatic, a high farce in the style of Molière. I thought it was brilliant, but it wasn't a Broadway-type show. After the performance I went back to see Dorothy and meet the birds. I was impressed by how well she cared for them. They were only two or three months old then and still needed to be hand-fed. I was amazed at how they had bonded to her. She would kiss them and pet them like they were little puppies. The training was much more complicated than I was used to with a dog. When I asked her where she had learned so much about birds, she said she was self-taught. Interesting, I thought, just like me. For a moment I was enjoying watching this woman show genuine affection for these creatures. Seeing the ease with which she handled them and the care and love she gave them, I thought given the proper training, she could easily be responsible for Bugsy.

Now, there were a couple of interesting things about training the dog for this show. First off, I was able to put some stipulations in the contract about the rehearsal time that I would need. Unlike shows in the past where getting the dog in would have the lowest priority, I made sure they put in writing that the dog would have high priority. I wanted guaranteed rehearsal time at least four times daily in a large space, plus stage time. I would have to rehearse once a day with the actor who played the prince. Dorothy would have to be available to work with me every day.

This production had a box set, which means that it had walls on the sides and in the back. Bugsy had to make her entrance every night through a door, which posed a problem because she would be in the wings behind the wall and wouldn't be able to see the shoe being thrown. We had to make sure the door was cracked open or that a hole was created so that she could see the shoe. She then would have to go out the door into this space, pick up the shoe in her mouth, bring it to the prince, drop it, and go back to where she had

"Who are you calling *La Bête?*"

entered. They agreed to my conditions, and I decided to stay.

In an effort to keep my training on *Annie Warbucks* going forward, I brought Chelsea with me. I wanted her to get used to the road, living in hotels and possibly getting onstage. I had the two dogs with me when I arrived in Boston in January to begin rehearsals. Because I was being brought in so late, the show had only two weeks left in the Boston run. I told them I would take most of those two weeks to get Bugsy ready and then show them the behavior onstage for the last two Boston performances. The first week I would train the dog onstage, the second week I would train the dog to listen to Dorothy. By the end of the second week, I would then step out so they could look at it and decide whether it worked and whether they wanted to bring it back to New York.

The first day of rehearsal I was ready to start working with Dorothy and Bugsy, only to find out Dorothy had to leave. Her mother and aunt had been in a very bad car accident. They had survived, but they were in the hospital and both in very bad shape. Dorothy had to rush back to

Connecticut because the doctors were worried that her mother might not survive. Because it was an emergency, I agreed to take care of the birds and handle the show while Dorothy was away. Dorothy and the producers were very grateful I was willing to help. Dorothy showed me the birds' medication, how to clean them, and how to feed them with an eyedropper—then she left to be with her family.

I wasn't familiar with large birds. (In fact, the only birds I had ever been around were the chickens in my Uncle Gino's backyard when I was a kid.) Cockatoos usually bond to the people who raise them, so Cicero and B were not happy that Dorothy wasn't there. They made their displeasure known to me. It was a really rocky start to taking care of them. I fed them, made sure they were clean, and got them to the theater. The stage managers helped get them onstage, but I was responsible for their care the rest of the time. I remember thinking, "I hardly know this woman and I'm already doing her job."

Dorothy's mother stabilized, so Dorothy was able to return to the theater after a few days. I was doing okay but was glad she was back. I had an even greater appreciation for her—she was obviously concerned but her mother insisted she go back to the show. That week I spent every day in the theater working with the director, the dog, and Dorothy. We worked on getting Bugsy into the pattern of entering from the door and deciding what object she would pick up. We would have her bring it to a person. We used stage managers, stagehands, anybody we could find as stand-ins, just to teach her the pattern. Dorothy would always be next to me while we did this. At first Bugsy was a little confused and reluctant, but then she started to get used to the pattern.

Besides spending four hours a day together in the theater, Dorothy and I got to go on a little road trip. Once I committed to the show, I needed an understudy. The press agent for the Wilbur Theater was a lovely woman named Nance Movsesian. She was one of the leading press agents in Boston and knew my rescue work from *Annie*. She helped me call around to the

Boston shelters for an understudy dog. We located another small, scruffy mix at the Animal Rescue League in Boston. When we met Nance to get the directions, she said, "You two are so cute, are you a couple?" It was one of those moments when you wonder, does this stranger know something I don't? Dorothy and I both laughed in an embarrassed way and went off.

We met the shelter manager who introduced us to Flicka, which is Swedish for "little girl." Flicka had been owned by an older lady who could no longer take care of her. She was about Bugsy's size but had more black on her, with a splash of white on her chest. She was friendly and outgoing. The shelter was very helpful, and we drove back with our new understudy. It's always a great feeling when you can save an animal, and I was glad Dorothy got the chance to experience it with me.

The dogs got along fine. Once Bugsy got used to the pattern, we started laying on the distractions, other people, more noise, and getting her used to the backstage area. At the end of that first week, I started showing Dorothy how to take care of Bugsy and how to run the cue. That transition proved to be bumpy because Bugsy had been working with me for almost two years, and now I was pretty much turning her over to a perfect stranger. But Dorothy persisted. She had a gentle way with Bugsy. The two of them had sleepovers, and by the middle of the last week, we were able to show the director the behavior. Bugsy would run onstage, grab the shoe, bring it to the prince, and then run off. Sometimes she would miss it and go to the prince and then go back and get it. Sometimes she would get the shoe and drop it two feet away from the prince. But the overall effect of a dog coming out of nowhere, doing something, and leaving is exactly what the director wanted. Dorothy had done an amazing job learning my methods, as well as taking care of the birds.

At that point the show closed in Boston and the cast went back to New York. I took the dogs back to Connecticut, repacked, and moved again, staying with Sarah Jessica Parker's family while we rehearsed for *Annie Warbucks*. Dorothy was staying with Wendy at her apartment, along with the

"Bugsy and I are both thinking, 'Nice bird.'"

two birds and the two small dogs. I remember helping Dorothy move the birds, cages, and dogs into the dressing room. We had had an intensive two weeks together and got along great.

By now, I realized that Dorothy was doing all of this mostly to help out her friend. In a way, we were alike. I had agreed to help people I knew and had worked with by training a dog. Dorothy and I had not studied animal training, but just used our natural love for animals. Even though she was not acting in it, it was Dorothy's first show on Broadway. I was glad I could share in that moment as well. Dorothy was so warm, sweet, loving, and hardworking that I was amazed guys weren't all over her.

The producers had Bugsy go on for the first two previews, and then exercised their option to cut the dog from the show and go ahead without me. The show opened four days later, and while it got some good reviews and a number of Tony Award nominations, it couldn't find an audience. It was a brilliant play that was brilliantly acted, but unfortunately, it couldn't run and the show closed. I thanked Dorothy for all of her hard work, both with Bugsy and with the birds, and we promised to remain friends and stay in contact. We had connected through the animals, and I discovered my intuition was right—she was a wonderful person, with no ulterior motives.

Later that year I was working on *Nick & Nora,* as well as other productions of *Annie* and *Annie Warbucks.* Dorothy would always find time to write. She was very good about staying in touch. She would come up to my house and visit Bugsy. I really liked her but didn't want to seem like I was leading her on in any way because I was dating someone else at the time. About four months after *La Bête* closed, I decided Flicka would be better off with a family. She was too excitable for show business. Dorothy mentioned her brother and sister-in-law were looking for a dog. She arranged for me to meet Jim and Ginger, who were living in a nice house in the country. They really took to Flicka and she took to them. They renamed her Mandy, and she lived with them for another fifteen years.

I again felt amazed that Dorothy had gone out of her way to help me and the little dog she helped rescue. She had a heart full of love. While I was out on the road with *Annie Warbucks,* I broke up with my girlfriend. I happened to be speaking to Dorothy one day and jokingly said, "Hey, I'm single again. If you find yourself out in Chicago in the next month, look me up." Imagine my surprise when she called the next weekend and said her cousin was a travel agent and had some travel vouchers. Dorothy could come to Chicago if the offer still stood. I remember thinking, This is too good to be true. I said I would love to see her.

Dorothy flew out and we had dinner before she saw the show. Afterward we walked and I really wanted to kiss her—but I respected her as a person and friend and didn't want to blow that, so I took it slow. I was like

a nervous teenager when I grabbed her hand as we walked. And she didn't take it away. She would often come out to visit me on the road, and we officially began dating.

When *Annie Warbucks* opened off-Broadway, I got her a job as the child supervisor so we could spend more time with each other. It felt good to be working together again. Soon after that, I asked her to move in with me in Connecticut. Sometime during 1994, while we were living together, she asked what I thought was a silly question. "If you could have any animal, what animal would you like?" We were having dinner at a restaurant and I said I thought llamas were funny. For my birthday that year she gave me a card with a gift certificate in it for two llamas. I was just blown away. We had been together for a while. She knew me and my imperfections. She knew that living with me meant living with dogs, cats, and all sorts of animals. Yet here she was, adding to this menagerie with a pair of unusual animals.

The gesture touched me so deeply that I asked her to marry me that Christmas Eve. We were married the next summer with the llamas in attendance. We have been working and living and taking care of animals together ever since.

Chapter 11

Outfoxed

Nick & Nora is remembered as one of the biggest flops in Broadway history. I remember it with fond memories of one smart little dog.

Back in 1987, two young producers contacted me about a new musical based on the *Thin Man* movies, those great old films that featured socialite detectives Nick and Nora Charles and their dog, Asta. They wanted Asta to be onstage throughout the play, just as he had been in the movies. The idea of an animal performing through an entire show was unprecedented—remember, until *Annie,* no one believed a dog could be depended on to play a character in a live production. I loved it. We began laying the groundwork for making that sort of performance possible. I got a call from the author, Arthur Laurents. We spoke, and he liked my input. The producers were very grateful and said they'd get back to me when the production was on its feet.

Four years later I saw an article in the *New York Post* about auditions for the role of Asta. It seems that there were new producers and new stars, Joanna Gleason and Barry Bostwick. Arthur Laurents was now directing as well. The music was by my old *Annie* colleague, Charles Strouse. It was going to be a major production. I called the producer's office and told them

Riley, Barry Bostwick, and Joanna Gleason in *Nick & Nora*. Photo by Photofest/Nathaniel Kramer

what my involvement had been. I was told another trainer had been hired, but I left my number just in case.

Months went by, and I kept reading about bad luck surrounding *Nick & Nora*—illness, money problems, creative differences—but nothing about the dog. In April 1991, I was in Tucson doing a production of *Annie* when I received a call from the producers. Things hadn't worked out with the other trainer. I explained that, based on my original discussions about the script, I would need a few months to train the dog. It would be close—rehearsals were to begin in August. My search began immediately. Wirehaired fox terriers, which are sometimes called "Asta" dogs, are small, white dogs with curly hair and very expressive faces. They were bred to be fast enough to chase foxes and intelligent enough to outsmart them. Past experiences with terriers made me worry about that last trait. Terriers in general are hard to train because of their independent nature, but there are certain breeds of terriers that are so independent, they are impossible to train for this type of work. I was afraid wirehaired terriers fell into this category.

Another challenge was that I needed a purebred dog, and they usually don't end up in shelters. I called some breeders in Arizona, looking for a rescue dog, and was put in touch with the Abandoned Terrier Rescue Association. It is a fox and Airedale terrier rescue kennel, run by Ruth Millington in Los Angeles County. I drove from Tucson to Ruth's ranch. There were terriers everywhere! It sounded like a battle zone when all those dogs started barking—I owned ten dogs at the time, and even I was taken aback.

We met a few dogs who were nice to strangers, then one little guy snuck through Ruth's legs, jumped up on the couch, and began sniffing my hair. His name was Riley. Riley had been a stray wandering the streets of Los Angeles, and his owner never claimed him at animal control, so Ruth went and got him. She named him Riley for being so lucky and now living "the life of Riley." He escaped almost all her barriers and did whatever he wanted. It frustrated and amused her that this dog always, well . . . outfoxed her. There was something about his all-out determination that made me laugh, too. After he finished sniffing my hair, he got down and wagged his tail and barked at me as if to say, "What took you so long to find me? Let's go!" He was pushy, but he had that certain something. I decided to take him and, if I had to, use him as an understudy.

I returned the next day to pick him up. From the minute we left the ranch, Riley started teaching me about fox terriers. Fortunately, I had purchased a carrier to transport him, just in case there were problems. He spent the first five minutes running around the van, literally bouncing off the walls. When I tried to hold him on my lap, he growled. I decided to put him in the carrier for safety. He didn't like the confinement of the van, and he liked the crate even less. He barked and growled the entire ten-hour drive back to Tucson. I thought he was upset about leaving the ranch, but I finally decided he was just plain angry he wasn't driving.

We made it back to Tucson just in time for the evening performance of *Annie*. I took the two Sandy dogs and left Riley with a friend. I thought he'd be tired from the ride. When I got home, Riley was running around the apartment, there was garbage everywhere, and my friend was locked in the bedroom. Riley spent his first night in the crate, barking. This dog was going to make Broadway history?

I had to make him accept that I was the alpha dog. He'd stare at me with piercing eyes and I'd stare back. In dog language, staring is a very threatening gesture, and it's usually only seconds before the weaker dog looks away. Riley would hold my gaze for a long time, and then his back leg would begin to shake, he'd growl, and, finally, he'd look away. I knew if I could harness that concentration for good instead of evil, he would be a great dog. When he finally accepted me as the alpha, he became one of the most attentive and smartest little dogs I had ever trained. But the first thing I had to do was make him understand that he had to do what *I* wanted before he got what *he* wanted.

The *Annie* production ended. The trip home took five days—the longest five days of my life. I called my answering machine from a phone booth in Oklahoma and got the message that the producers of *Nick & Nora* had found a less-expensive trainer—someone with a Hollywood reputation. I could hear Riley barking from the van, and each bark shot through my nerves like fingernails on a chalkboard. After all the time, energy, and money I had invested in this project, I was excused without so much as a thank-you. I was furious. This time when I told Riley to be quiet, he listened. He must have heard the angst in my voice—he was not going to mess with me. I thought about placing him in a home, but I couldn't imagine anyone capable of handling him. Even though I had lost lots of sleep, I enjoyed the challenge Riley presented. I felt I owed him the chance to live with me like all the others after their shows closed. Talk about the life of Riley! He hadn't even worked and he was retiring.

I began the process of training him to make him a better pet, and I decided to use his intelligence against him. I was going to make him believe that obeying me was his idea. I had other dogs do behaviors in front of him—then they'd get rewarded and he'd get nothing. It didn't take him long to figure out what he had to do to beat the other dogs out of the treat. The more he obeyed, the more attention he got from me. From then on we were able to work things out.

By August 1991 preliminary rehearsals had begun for *Nick & Nora,* and their latest dog tried to bite Barry Bostwick. They were only eight weeks away from the first performance. Arthur Laurents gave the producers an ultimatum: get a dog that works or else. The producers came back to me. This time, I told them I would do it, but I raised my fee substantially. When they accepted, I realized I had proven to the Broadway community that I was the go-to guy for animals. Even a big Hollywood trainer couldn't do what I was able to achieve.

Arthur and I went through the script together. When we got to the last scenes, Arthur said he wanted Asta to bring on the clue that solved the murder. I said, "Do you really want the resolution of the entire show to rely on an animal?" He looked me straight in the eye and said, "Yes." I left the meeting fully aware of the challenge I faced. Rehearsals began in seven days, I had a maniac dog I'd just figured out how to train, I had no understudy dog, and this was the most ambitious project I'd ever undertaken. So

I immediately began work on the final trick. Asta was to bring on a watch that belonged to the murder victim and give it to Nora. That clue helps reveal the murderer. Terriers are not known for fetching—that's for retrievers. If I threw a toy, Riley would make *me* go get it. If I put a watch in his mouth, he'd spit it out. So I got my best retrieving dog and began throwing my watch around the living room and rewarding the dog for bringing it back. Not to be upstaged, Riley caught on in no time. I thought we might have a shot.

I began searching for an understudy. People always laugh when I tell them I have understudy dogs, but every actor in a show has someone to back them up in case of emergency. From the very first Sandy until now, I have always had a backup dog, but my secret hope is that they never go on. In a high-pressure situation like a Broadway show, there's barely time to get one dog up to speed, never mind two.

My contacts in the Humane Society of New York led me to a farmer in New Jersey who had acquired a wirehaired fox terrier for breeding, but never got around to it. He had left the dog tied up in his barn all winter—when he ran out of dog food, he gave it horse feed. When I met BJ, he was emaciated and his coat was matted. After a year of isolation, you can imagine this dog's joy when I gave him some biscuits and a hug. BJ sank right into my arms—the only thing moving was his little cropped tail. The farmer offered to give me the dog, but I paid five dollars for him and got a receipt, just to make it legal. BJ jumped into my van and never looked back. He went directly to my vet for medical attention and quarantine—he had every worm in the book and had to eat special food until his digestive system could tolerate dog food again.

In my meeting with the company, I was very candid. I explained we were behind in training and that these dogs could be aggressive and unpredictable. I asked for everyone's cooperation and assistance, and I got it. From the stars to the stage managers, everyone was wonderful. They helped me socialize Riley and get him used to a lot of people, and they gave both dogs love, which they desperately needed. My main job was to bond Riley to

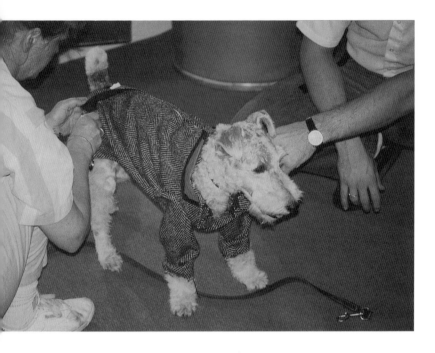

"Does this make my tail look too big?"

Barry and Joanna. They would be the ones commanding him, and he had to love them—or at least act like he did onstage. At first, both actors were apprehensive about having to spend all their free time with Riley—after all, they had the success of a new musical riding on their shoulders. But both are animal lovers and found a way to give me all they could. Only real professionals extend themselves as much as they did. As Riley got used to the company and BJ started learning the basics, the dog department was going more smoothly than any other. Arthur was so pleased with our progress that he added Riley to more scenes as rehearsals went on.

My next worry was getting Riley used to the noise and chaos, both backstage and in front of the audience—a problem when you spend so much time in a rehearsal hall. Thanks to several stage managers and my old friends in the stagehands' union, Riley and I were able to hang out backstage at currently running shows. At *Cats*, he wanted to chase those big animals, but he restrained himself and adjusted quickly. When a dog gets bored enough to lay down backstage or in the orchestra pit, he's used to the sights and sounds of the theater.

I also began working on the understudy. BJ was a nice dog and was recovering well, but he was barely housebroken and knew very few commands. He worked hard, and little by little he learned basic obedience. One stage manager, Mo Gibson, always felt sorry for him and gave him extra attention, which came in very handy later on. As rehearsals continued, I was still worried about the watch trick. I knew that Riley would try to do it right every night, but there was always a chance he wouldn't, so I came up with a backup plan. I rigged an extra watch onstage in case Riley had a problem.

We finally moved to the Marriott Marquis on Times Square for the beginning of technical rehearsals. My contract called for a private dressing room for the dogs, both for safety and so they could rest. We had such a large cast that all the dressing rooms were taken. I was arguing with the management over my dressing room when Arthur offered us his. Arthur Laurents is a brilliant writer and director with a legendary temper, but he was always kind and understanding with the dogs and me. He listened to my suggestions and either agreed or worked with me to solve problems. My work with him on *Nick & Nora* remains one of my most pleasant experiences with a director.

But the word on the street was that the show was having terrible troubles, and to some extent it was true. The computerized set was groundbreaking but flawed. There were cast replacements and illnesses. In addition, the storyline was very dark—not what you expect in a Broadway musical, especially one based on a very popular film series. Changes in the script and music were coming fast and furious.

The big watch trick, on the other hand, was proceeding very well, with a 100 percent success rate. At the top of that final scene, Joanna would get a piece of cheese offstage. Riley would carry the watch in and trade with Joanna for the cheese. In his mind, he was getting the better end of the bargain. Then he would go off to Mo, stage left. But we soon found out why it was a good thing I had a backup plan. During dress rehearsal, the watch slipped out of Riley's mouth. This had happened now and then in rehearsals, but he'd just pick it up and continue. This time it fell directly through one of the quarter-inch tracks on the stage used for the moving scenery. Riley began digging at the floor to get it back, but Joanna had the presence of mind to give him the cheese, send him off, and pick up the spare watch I had hidden behind the wall. Arthur later thanked me for thinking ahead.

Finally, we began previews. In the old days, you took the show on the road to work out all the bugs before you came to New York, but in the last twenty years, that process has become too expensive. So producers take the big risk of opening in New York. The audience loved parts of the show, and Riley was one of those parts. Arthur and the creators worked to fix the others.

I always ask the people involved to inform me when any new element is being introduced to the pattern of the show. An actor, prop, costume, sound or line change—any change in the set routine will distract the animal. This time, a change was made in previews, and they didn't tell me. Joanna Gleason is a vegetarian and won't wear fur. But our designer, Theoni Aldredge, felt a socialite like Nora should wear a fox stole in one of the scenes. Joanna refused. Unless an actor has refusal over costumes in her contract, she is obligated to wear whatever the designer assigns. It was a battle of wills in which neither woman would budge.

Arthur stepped in and persuaded Joanna to wear it for one performance so he could look at it and make the final decision. No one told me. The scene was entitled "Walking the Dog." Nick and Nora take Asta for his evening walk. Each evening I met Barry stage left, handed him Riley's leash, and went stage right to wait for them to exit. That night when I got to my position, I saw Riley growl and leap at Joanna! I couldn't see Joanna, but I could see Barry trying to pull Riley off her. In that moment I saw my career and everything I owned going down the drain. None of my animals has ever bitten an actor, let alone in front of an audience. The moment went on forever.

Barry finally got Riley detached and they started the number. Barry and Joanna were trying to sing but they couldn't stop laughing, Riley was growling and barking, and the audience was in stitches. The number finally ended and they all exited. As I frantically tried to see if Joanna was hurt, apologizing the whole time, she threw her arms around me and thanked me for helping her with her problem. What I couldn't see from the wings was that Riley had attacked the stole. He is a fox terrier—he saw a fox wrapped around Joanna's neck, its beady little eyes staring at him, and he tried to kill it. Although I had no clue from my vantage point, the very amused audience could plainly see what was happening. All furs were banned from the show, and no new elements were added to Riley's scenes without informing me.

There was one more incident before the opening. One Saturday night, I was walking the dogs after the show when Riley began limping. I inspected him but didn't find anything wrong. I was sure it was nothing and went to bed. The next morning Riley refused to walk and seemed to be in terrible pain. Fox terriers are very tough—so this meant something serious. I called our stage manager friend, Mo Gibson, and told her the situation. She met me at the Animal Medical Center, one of the finest veterinary facilities in the world. Given the urgency of the situation, they put their best people on it, but they couldn't find a cause for the lameness. The doctors told me they would need to run more tests. It was about noon, and Mo reminded me we had a matinee at two. She assured me Riley was in good hands and that we had to get BJ ready to go on. Those words sent a cold chill up my spine. Not the understudy!

When an understudy goes on, it is a very exciting experience. It's a chance for an unknown to shine. The cast was thrilled, but I was scared to death. BJ knew the behaviors, but he'd never encountered the presence of an audience. He could notice them and ignore them. He could notice them and feel the need to scare them out of his theater. Or, he could notice them and want to say hello to every one of them. That's what I was afraid he'd do.

The show opens outside Nick and Nora's apartment. The set revolves, and we see Asta on the other side of the door, waiting for them to come home. During the following scene change, the dog had one safe path through the computerized, moving set to come to me, where I stood about thirty feet away in the wings. BJ had no problem with the revolving set. When his cue came to exit, he stepped toward me. Then he heard the audience applaud his entrance and stopped. He looked at them, he wagged his tail, he stood there, happy as could be. I was thrilled that the audience didn't upset him, but he was missing his safe exit, and if he stayed where he was, the set would literally run him over. He couldn't hear my commands over the orchestra and applause, and I thought he was doomed. Thinking quickly, Mo Gibson appeared stage right about ten feet away from him,

and called him. He saw her and, because of their offstage relationship, trotted toward her just in time. The rest of the performance went all right. The final cue with the watch didn't work, but Joanna covered it. I couldn't thank Mo enough for being there to help me and for saving BJ's life. There are true artists in this business, and they don't always appear onstage. We went back to the hospital after the show to check in on Riley. They'd discovered a sliver of glass in his paw. Once it was removed, Riley was as good as new.

The show finally opened. After the rough previews, we all knew what was coming. The reviews were bad and it closed in a week. Many reviewers will praise an animal's performance in order

Ready for rehearsal.

to ridicule or insult the work of the human performers and creators and this happened with *Nick & Nora*. Riley received some of the best reviews of the show. The *New York Observer* went so far as to say the show was so bad that Asta was put to sleep after it closed. Although it was supposed to be a joke, it took quite a while for me to convince everyone from the show and the theatrical community that Riley was alive and living on my farm.

I was very proud of both those dogs. When the show closed, I could think of no happier ending for BJ than to give him to Mo. He was a great pet. He was not as smart or good-looking as Riley, but he played the role of loving dog for many years. Riley spent many years running my house. All my dogs are welcome to live out their lives on the farm, but some have a hard time adjusting. During a show they are top dog, loved and adored by all. Then they come home with me and are part of the pack. The smart ones like Riley know the difference.

In 1998 I did a children's production of *The Wizard of Oz*. Since all my "Totos" were out on the road, I used Riley. He loved being back onstage again. Rehearsals went fine, but during the dress rehearsal he got very interested in the Lion. He contained himself for about a week, then one night, when the Lion was chasing Dorothy, he ran up and bit the actor right on the tail. Fortunately, it was a thick costume and the actor was fine. The actor playing the Scarecrow thought it was the funniest thing he'd ever seen. He said he would love to have a dog like Riley. He was married to a writer, and they didn't have any children and had been looking for a dog, so they adopted him. He was back to being a star.

Chapter 12

Annie Gets Her Walking Papers

The 1990s were proving to be an interesting decade. *Annie Warbucks* ended up closing at the end of January 1994, after running for 200 performances. With *La Bête* and *Nick & Nora*, I added another two Broadway credits to my résumé. I had rescued seven more dogs. In 1994 and 1995, I continued to work in regional theater, small tours, and films. The best part of 1995 was getting married to Dorothy in July.

There are good things and bad things about marrying an animal trainer. One of the bad things is living with the mess, but one of the good things was being able to get any animal you want, within reason. Dorothy had always wanted a white Arabian horse, so instead of a big fancy wedding, we got married in our backyard under a beautiful tent and registered at Home Depot for the materials we needed to build a barn. By Labor Day 1995, we had our first two horses. Dorothy had found a job at the Bushnell Memorial Theater in Hartford as the personal assistant to the executive director. Life was good.

In December 1995 I got a call from Roger Hess, a producer who had optioned the rights for a twentieth-anniversary revival of *Annie*. His plan was for a tour that would end up in New York, twenty years after Annie had originally opened. We had a nice chat, and he explained that they were

Joanna Pacitti, as Annie, with Zappa in the 20th Anniversary production of *Annie*. *Photo by Carol Rosegg*

planning to publicize and market the tour to maximize profits. I sent him an information sheet on how our agency works, and he said they would be in touch.

In the spring of 1996 I adopted a dog from a shelter in Rhode Island. His name was Zappa, after Frank Zappa, the rock star. He was the largest Sandy dog we had ever had—most dogs we used were around 60 pounds, but Zappa was over 80 pounds. Martin Charnin had always wanted an Irish wolfhound–sized dog, but that would have been impractical. Zappa was a slow-moving, gentle giant—not very excitable. He just wanted to lie around and be petted. Cindy Lou had easily learned *Annie*, as well as *Annie Warbucks*, and was performing in productions around the country. We also had two other dogs, Sparky and Cosmo, working in other small productions. Martin Charnin was going to direct a separate *Annie* revival at Goodspeed in 1996 as well as the tour, which would open on Broadway in 1997. We set up Sparky and Cosmo to do the Goodspeed run. There was something nice about coming back to the theater where I had originally begun, to re-create the work that started my career.

During the summer of 1996, two things were decided—the producers of the tour took a poll of all the theaters around the country who would book the show to see who they would like to see in the role of Miss Hannigan. Nell Carter was the number-one choice. For the first time in the history of *Annie*, an actor's name would appear above the title. They even wrote a new song for her. The second thing was that the producers partnered with Macy's department stores to hold a nationwide search for the actress to play Annie. Auditions were held all summer in stores around the country. Andrea McArdle and Zappa were there to announce the winner at Macy's in New York City.

ABC's show *Turning Point* was given unprecedented access to film the whole procedure, from the first auditions to the first performance in Houston, Texas. *Turning Point* even came to our house to film the training process we used with the dogs. They were there the moment the winner was announced, an eleven-year-old girl from Philadelphia named Joanna

Pacitti. Her family was working class—her dad, Joe, owned a barbershop in the basement of their home; her mom, Stella; and two older sisters. It was a real-life Cinderella story for Joanna. The search generated photo shoots, interviews, and a lot of attention for a show that was having its twenty-year revival.

Rehearsals began in New York in October 1996. Even though Joanna only weighed 50 pounds to Zappa's 80, she worked really well with him, and they formed a true bond. We went to Houston in November, and Dorothy decided to leave her job to travel with me and act as the kids' chaperone. We thought we would work together to save some money for starting a family. ABC was still there, filming every day, and they were backstage for the tech rehearsals and for the first performance. This was Zappa's first time onstage with an audience, and he didn't do all his tricks exactly right. At the end of the show Sandy is supposed to come out in a big Christmas box. For some reason Zappa wouldn't go into the box, so ABC filmed me crawling into the box with him and being wheeled onstage. During dress rehearsal, one of our actresses had a seizure. I knew CPR from leaner days when I worked at a hospital between gigs, so I was able to take care of her until the ambulance arrived. All of this drama was caught on film.

The show opened to the typical warm reception it always received. Nell Carter was Miss Hannigan, and Conrad John Schuck was Daddy Warbucks. John had played the role on Broadway fifteen years earlier, and now he was re-creating it for the tour. Dorothy and I traveled in a van we had bought, and we had a lot of the comforts of home. We would cook meals for the cast in our hotel room. After we finished the Houston run, our next stop was Minneapolis, where we spent Christmas. It was freezing cold, but I went out in a blizzard and found a Christmas tree and surprised the kids.

The ABC special was supposed to air in November but was postponed. On the air date in December, it was bumped for coverage of Frank Sinatra's death. It didn't matter to us in the cast—we were getting great reviews. We played a week in Chicago and then three weeks in Baltimore, followed by two weeks in Boston. While we were in Boston something strange happened. When we had started rehearsals, a little girl named Alexandra had been chosen to understudy Annie and the other orphans. I had been training her all along. In Boston I was taken aside and told to secretly rehearse another orphan for the role, Brittny Kissinger. I was told not to question the decision and to keep it private. Brittny was very sweet, but even smaller than Joanna—much too small to work with Zappa, so we rehearsed her with Cindy Lou, who was accomplished in the role.

In Boston, Joanna became ill and missed a couple of shows. Alexandra went on for the first time. Then it was announced that Brittny was going to go on, to see how she did in the role. Alexandra was upset because she had been preparing for the role as the understudy and couldn't understand what was going on. The ABC special had finally aired in February, and people all around the country were very excited about the show. We all did our jobs professionally and Brittny went on with Cindy Lou, even though it made many people in the cast upset.

Our next stop was Hershey, Pennsylvania. There we were told that Brittny and Joanna would be splitting the role—but that Brittny would be opening for the critics in New York. Joanna's agents were very upset and busy trying to get to the bottom of why this change had been made. Joanna's family refused to take the deal. Her contract said she would be playing Annie on Broadway. Joanna had been getting good reviews, so no one in the cast understood why she was being asked to step down. Brittny was a sweet kid being thrust into the middle of a controversy that she and her family had never asked for. The kids were crying, the cast was very upset, and we were eight weeks away from opening on Broadway.

The ultimatum to Joanna came at the end of the week in Hershey. Our next stop was Wallingford, Connecticut, for one week. Dorothy and I couldn't wait to get home and away from all the drama. The company took a bus, but we drove home in our van. At 1:00 A.M. on Monday morning, our phone rang. It was Stella, Joanna's mother, and she was crying hysterically. A note had been pushed under their hotel room door saying Joanna was being released from her contract and a car would pick them up at 8:00 A.M. to drive them back to Philadelphia. They were calling me for advice. After years of experience with *Annie* and *Annie Warbucks*, I always worry about kids in show business. The rejection and backstage gossip can be devastating, and I've seen too many kids who were pushed into performing and didn't really want to be there. When I worked in the hospital, I had worked in the psychiatric ward with suicidal and abused kids. I felt that if Joanna was to come out of this intact, she needed some control and some closure.

I told Stella, "You have to leave, but let's do it on your terms." We would pick them up and bring them to our house. Joanna could play with the animals and take her mind off of all the problems with the show. In the morning she could tell us who she wanted to say good-bye to, and then they could go home—and that's exactly what we did. At 2:00 A.M., Dorothy and I snuck Joanna and Stella out of their hotel room and brought them to our house. Joanna got to sleep with Zappa one more time. In the morning Joanna gave us a list of the people she wanted to say good-bye to. We found another hotel in the area and got them a room there. I called a child psychiatrist and a nurse who were friends of mine from my old job at the hospital, to help her process the good-byes. We secretly shuttled cast members to the location, and at 2:00 P.M., we put Joanna and Stella in a car to go home.

You can only imagine the company's panic when they went to the hotel room where the Pacittis were supposed to be at 8:00 A.M., only to find they had checked out. Our call at the theater that day was 6:30 P.M. Our producer called a meeting. Half of the cast knew about Joanna and the other half didn't. When he announced that Joanna had left and Brittny was taking over, many people cried. When he said Joanna was doing well and sent her regards, half of the cast knew it wasn't true. I asked if I could say a few words. I stood up and told the cast that Dorothy and I had spent the night with the Pacittis, that they sent their love, and that they were on their way home.

No one wanted Brittny to fail, so we all went on to do the show that night, and did our job well. It's a cliché about the theater being a family, but it's true. When someone leaves a company, particularly under circumstances like these, it takes a big toll on the spirit of the show. Many of us pursued the reason for the firing with the company and the unions, but we were told just to let it go. ABC, meanwhile, was very angry. They had run their special just two weeks before and now felt the firing made them look foolish. National publicity about the incident generated a lot of sympathy for Joanna. She was brought on shows like *Rosie*, ABC did a follow-up special on her, and there was news coverage all over about the Annie who was fired four weeks before opening on Broadway.

A happy ending; a girl and her dog.

The "official" word was that Joanna didn't have what it takes to make it on Broadway, but Brittny did. Rumors circulated that the producer was hoping to generate the same kind of buzz that happened when Andrea McArdle replaced Kristen Vigard in the original production. If that's what they were hoping, it backfired. The delay of the ABC special meant everything happened too close to the Broadway opening, and the publicity was bad.

Our next town was Montreal. There were seven of us who were furious over the way the whole thing had been handled. When we got to Montreal, we were each brought into management's office and told that if we continued our protesting, we would be fired. No good reason was given. We affectionately called ourselves the

Montreal Seven. At about this time, just as the tour was coming to an end, Dorothy and I found out we were going to become parents. It was a shining light in a very difficult time.

Although Brittny had been working with Zappa, he really missed Joanna. With my first child on the way, I wondered what I would do if my daughter was hurting as badly as Joanna. At the end of the Montreal run, we drove back home on a Monday, and the next day Dorothy and I drove to Philadelphia and surprised Joanna by giving her Zappa. She fell on the ground and hugged that dog in an embrace like I had never seen. Her mother said, "Bill, you can't do this; they'll fire you." What she didn't know was that my contract stipulated I had to "provide a trained dog to play the role of Sandy." It didn't specify *which* dog. Cindy Lou was accomplished and had worked with Brittny, so I knew the performance wouldn't suffer—but Joanna deserved something no Annie had ever had: a Sandy that would be her own personal dog.

Brittny Kissinger, here with Cindy Lou, got her chance to shine as Annie. *Photo by Sara Krulwich/ The New York Times/ Redux*

By the time we reached Broadway, there was still a cloud over the show. We didn't get the kind of press coverage or reviews the producers expected. Many members of the original cast who had been invited to attend as part of the anniversary boycotted the opening. I tried to find something to make a bad situation better. I came up with an idea that I thought would generate good publicity and help animals at the same time. Right before Sandy comes on in the show, there's a scene called "The Stray Mutt." While Annie is standing on the street, a dogcatcher walks by carrying a dog he says he's taking to the pound. I had actually asked the creators to write this scene into the original production—it was a way to get our understudy onstage to prep him in case he had to go on.

In this production, our other understudy, Sparky, already had experience. I thought, What if we could get the Humane Society to bring over a dog a week, let us carry it on, and make an announcement that it was up for adoption? I contacted the Humane Society of New York, which is a no-kill shelter in the city that I had been helping for more than twenty years. They jumped at the chance. So for the twenty-six weeks we ran on Broadway, an announcement was made before each show that said, "The role of the Stray Mutt will be played by so-and-so, who will be available for adoption from the Humane Society of New York in the lobby during intermission." It would get a great round of applause right before the overture started. My Stray Mutt program was a huge success. Twenty-six dogs were featured, and many more went home with great families. The Humane Society took applications at intermission, and their adoptions increased by 200 percent. We were back in the good graces of the press.

In October the show closed on Broadway due to lack of business and went back on tour, but Dorothy and I didn't go with it. Our small two-bedroom house was already overcrowded with fifteen animals—there was no room for a baby. In August we had the roof torn off and we added a second story. We lived in a small guesthouse in the back. We finished construction three weeks before our daughter, Jenna, was born in November 1997.

Something about being a dad made me even more protective about kids. During the summer of the Broadway run, I had arranged for Joanna and Zappa to do a production of *Annie* at the North Carolina Theater—the last theater that the original Sandy had ever seen. She went on to a lucrative recording deal and has a CD of her music out now. Unfortunately, it was a while before the unpleasantness completely ended. Joanna's family sued Macy's, because the contract they had signed at the audition guaranteed Joanna would play Annie on Broadway. The day before the trial was slated to start, they reached a settlement. Terms were never revealed, and we still don't know the real reason why Joanna was fired. All I know is that Zappa lived a happy life with the Pacittis until his natural death, we managed to save a number of homeless dogs, and I became a father—so I guess the twentieth-anniversary production of *Annie* had its good side, too.

Joanna—the consummate Annie.
Photo by Carol Rosegg

Chapter 13

We're Off to See Roseanne?

In May 1993 we were contacted by Theater by the Sea, a small theater in Matunuck, Rhode Island—they were doing a summer stock production of *The Wizard of Oz*. Throughout the 80s, I got occasional calls about productions of *Oz*, but it's a difficult show to do because of all the special scenic effects, so a lot of smaller theaters aren't interested in producing it. When I did get a call to do it, I'd send out Bugsy, my little schnauzer mix.

We had a trainer in Rhode Island who was interested in doing this production because it would be close to home for her. But, by then, Bugsy was too old to do the role, and I didn't have a "Toto" dog. In the L. Frank Baum book, Toto is a Scottie, but in the movie they used a cairn terrier, so that's what everyone thinks Toto should be. We tried searching pounds, but in the short amount of time we had—performances were going to start in June—we weren't able to find one. As we have done in similar cases, we contacted the breed rescue organization, a wonderful resource when you want a purebred dog. Through them we found a breeder in Holyoke, Massachusetts, who had a six-year-old female named Plenty that she was willing to sell to us. We purchased Plenty and trained her in a month to do the summer stock production. We also had her grandfather, Wolfy, as the understudy.

The production was so popular that this little theater put together a non-Equity tour that traveled the country from 1993 to 1994. Breed rescue

Roseanne, as the Wicked Witch of the West, in *The Wizard of Oz*. *Photo courtesy of Michael Gruber*

put us in touch with a breeder in southern New Jersey. Max was eight years old and no longer producing as a sire, so we bought him. Plenty and Max were very sweet, very calm, and did well in that tour.

When Dorothy moved to Connecticut in 1994, I had fourteen dogs. I had acquired them all, they lived with me, and they all pretty much ignored her—except Plenty, who really became her dog. She was the dog that followed Dorothy around and slept on her side of the bed, so Dorothy felt she had her own dog in the midst of this pack. When we decided to go out on tour with the twentieth-anniversary revival of *Annie,* Dorothy was upset that she would be away from Plenty for such a long time. The solution was simple—if we were going to travel with two big Sandy dogs, why couldn't we travel with one more little cairn terrier? So we did. Plenty came with us on the national tour of *Annie* before it came into New York. She was great to travel with. Her only problem was when we were in Minneapolis for Christmas it was 15 degrees below zero, and she refused to go outside in the cold weather—we thought she was going to burst! But other than that, Plenty was a joy to have on the road.

In January 1997 we heard that Madison Square Garden was mounting a huge production of *The Wizard of Oz.* It was going to be a revival of a production that was done out at the Paper Mill Playhouse, the state theater for New Jersey. I've worked there a number of times over the years. When Paper Mill did *The Wizard of Oz,* they hired a local dog trainer to come in with a little black dog to play Toto. While the dog was fine for that production, the plan was to greatly expand the show for New York and make it much more like the movie. We contacted them and they were very interested in our services.

We set up a meeting with the director in New York City. The only day we could do it was the day that we were traveling between Baltimore and Boston for the *Annie* anniversary tour in early February. It was fate that we had Plenty with us and that New York was on our way during that trip. We left Baltimore, came in, met the director, and showed them what Plenty could do. He was very impressed and very interested in working with us. Rehearsals were going to begin in New York in April. One of the things he stressed, though, was that he really wanted to make the play resemble the film. By that he meant that he wanted Toto to be onstage in every scene, just as she is in the film.

By that time, in my twenty years of providing animals for the theater, the only thing that came close to this was *Nick & Nora*, where Asta was onstage more than any other dog I had trained. But Toto has to perform a wide variety of actions, from sitting quietly in a handbasket to escaping from the witch's castle. It was clear to me that while we could train one dog to do a lot of things, we couldn't get one dog to do the number of things that were needed for this particular production. I proposed training two dogs that looked alike to play the role—one dog that would be calm and quiet, and another dog to do the action scenes. Plenty, who was younger than Max, would be the action dog, and Max, although he was a little bigger and a little grayer, would be the quiet dog.

With all the problems that had been associated with the anniversary production of *Annie*, plus the fact that Dorothy really loved Plenty, she asked if she could be the trainer on *The Wizard of Oz*. I couldn't think of anyone better to handle a show of this magnitude for me, and to handle it in a way that I was accustomed to. We worked side by side preparing Plenty and Max, but she never got the credit for it in the press like I did. Dorothy gave her notice to the *Annie* producer before the show came into New York, so that she could be free to start rehearsals for *Oz* in April.

I did have one concern—Dorothy was in the first trimester of her pregnancy. But she insisted she could easily handle the limited run of sixteen weeks, and no one would ever have to know. She also insisted I not tell a soul for fear they wouldn't hire her. We began an intensive rehearsal period, trying to devise a way to have an animal play a character onstage for the entire show. This was an expensive show to produce because of the large set and all the special effects. Plus, the run was going to be limited, meaning less chance for the producers to get a return on their investment. So, first they decided they would do twelve shows a week, compared to eight a week on Broadway, at a discounted price. Then they also made a bold casting move—they decided to hire Roseanne Barr to play the Wicked Witch of the West. Roseanne had just completed nine successful years with her sitcom. No one could figure out why she would want to come to Broadway and work for a fraction of the money that she could make in Hollywood, but she did.

Now, as I've said, what's great about the theater is that there's generally a real sense of family—we're colleagues, we all work together, and we all live together. My experience with films and television is just the opposite. You come in, you do the job, and you get out. When we first met her, you could see that's where Roseanne was coming from—she was surrounded by bodyguards, dressers, personal assistants, had to have a private dressing room at the rehearsal room, and stayed to herself. Plus, Roseanne had been taking a lot of criticism for some of the choices she had made in her career, so I think she thought she would be meeting that same sort of resistance when she came to work on Broadway. Along the way, we also found out Roseanne had never done a live show before—she had done stand-up, of course, but this would be her theatrical debut, so she was nervous. Slowly but surely, as Roseanne got a chance to work with this cast and crew, she realized that none of that mattered. We didn't care who she was or what she had done before—we were all there to do a job, and we were all pulling for her. By the time we opened, she'd warmed up and was a funny and gracious person to work with.

For this production they also held a nationwide search for the role of Dorothy. After auditioning more than 300 girls, they found fifteen-year-old high-school student Jessica Grové, born and bred in Columbus, Ohio. She had a presence, an innocence, and sincerity that were appealing, and a voice that was just unbelievable. They brought her to New York and introduced her at a press conference at the Rainbow Room, where she sang "Over the Rainbow." Also in the cast were Ken Page as the Lion, Michael Gruber as the Tin Man, and Lara Teeter as the Scarecrow—three very accomplished Broadway character actors.

While a lot of the cast and crew came from the Paper Mill production, many people were new, and there was a growing excitement as we went into rehearsal. Each year Madison Square Garden had been successful in presenting a production of *A Christmas Carol,* which became an annual event for many families. Their idea was to take one of America's most beloved stories, *The Wizard of Oz,* and make it an annual event for the summer. There was a lot of publicity leading up to the opening. But we worried whether a 15-year-old could learn how to do the role, sustain the role with Broadway veterans, and handle two dogs at one time. This young actress, Jessica Grové, was just amazing. Her sweetness and kindness were real. She loved the dogs, and she worked on her own time, both in rehearsal and out, to make these dogs love her and to perform the necessary behaviors.

There was one other unusual challenge about this show—we would be trying to re-create moments from a beloved film that most of the audience would have engrained in their memories. It was our job to be true to those memories. For example, the movie opens with Dorothy running home with Toto close behind her. To achieve that, Jessica would show Plenty a treat, then run out onstage with Plenty close behind. My favorite part was during "Over the Rainbow." In the film, after Judy Garland sings the first chorus, she walks over to a piece of farm machinery, where Toto is waiting, and the dog extends her paw toward the girl. I wanted to capture that small gesture—and it actually proved to be pretty simple, using Plenty's natural reaction. After sitting quietly for most of the song, Plenty was pretty bored. So when Jessica approached her, she naturally put out her paw, as though to say, "Let's do something already." But to the audience, it was that moment when Dorothy's closest friend tries to console her. It got a reaction from the audience every night.

The very next scene also has a favorite moment, when Toto steals Professor Marvel's hot dog. That was Plenty's favorite scene. All we had to do was keep her in Jessica's arms until the right moment, then put her down—Plenty would run over and grab the hot dog with no prompting. When Mickey Rooney took over the role of Professor Marvel, of course he turned this into a bit. Instead of letting Plenty get the hot dog, he would carry it around with him while she jumped after him, much to the audience's delight.

There's an example like that in almost every scene, from when they meet Glinda the Good Witch to the moment when Dorothy wakes up in her bed and says, "There's no place like home." The only place where we deliberately changed a scene is when Professor Marvel is revealed as the Wizard. Unlike in the movie, where Toto pulls the curtain open, in our version Toto just went under the curtain and started barking. For those *Wizard of Oz* fanatics who think Toto pulls the curtain open, if you look closely, you'll see that the curtain is tied to the neck of the dog. When I pointed this out to our director, he laughed and said, "Well, she can just go under the curtain, then."

The show opened in May 1997. Madison Square Garden threw a huge opening-night party with searchlights and hundreds of guests. The show ran until June, and during that time, over 200,000 people came to see it. It was an immediate success. I got a huge chuckle out of the *New York Times*

Jessica Grové, Plenty, and the cast of *The Wizard of Oz.*

review. In a very positive review of the show, this is what they said about Toto: "Move over, Sandy, there is a new canine star in town." How cool is it to have two of your own dogs competing for reviews in the *New York Times*?

Roseanne had come to enjoy the theater and being part of this cast so much that her dressing-room door was always open, and she invited people in to hang out with her. Jessica, Plenty, and Max became a real team. Jessica, at fifteen years old and with that remarkable presence, always kept the dogs on their marks and the show moving forward. She really held her own with the Broadway veterans she was working with in the cast. And, of course, my wife Dorothy came through with flying colors—but everyone kept trying to give me the credit.

Because of the show's popularity, Madison Square Garden decided to bring it back for the summer of 1998. They also reworked it so that it would be able to tour. That was a challenge, because the set had been designed for the large stages at Paper Mill and Madison Square Garden and was filled with special effects, from pyrotechnics to flying. They had to revamp it so that it would be easy to move. In February 1998 we were reassembled to start rehearsing for the national tour—except this time, it starred Eartha Kitt as the Wicked Witch of the West and Mickey Rooney as the Wizard. We rehearsed for a month, then went to Chicago and Detroit before coming back to New York for a limited run, from late April to the end of May. Then it went out on the road for another year.

Dorothy, Toto, and the Tin Man mug for the camera.
Photo courtesy of Michael Gruber

By then our daughter had been born, and as much as Dorothy wanted to, she wasn't able to travel. Max retired after his first year of performing. He had started to slow down, so he went to live with my mom as a pampered pet for the rest of his life. We went back to the breeder, who had a five-year-old dog she was willing to give up. Ashley had stopped producing puppies, so it wasn't worth it for the breeder to keep her. She had been overbred, which depleted the calcium in her body, so she had brittle bones and bad teeth—and very bad breath. But she was a very sweet girl and went out with Plenty for a great tour.

Eartha Kitt in the 1990s was in her seventies, but the energy and spirit she had as a performer was amazing to be around. Mickey Rooney always had a funny joke and a smile on his face—but you could never be certain what he was going to do next. Onstage he might ham it up or even improvise, which made it very difficult for the other actors. But whatever he did, the audiences loved him. All in all, the extended eighteen-month tour of *The Wizard of Oz* brought joy to many people around the country. Even though Madison Square Garden was not Broadway, this was still a major New York show that marked yet another turning point in my career—we proved to everyone in New York that we could take a dog and turn it into a character that could be onstage for an entire evening.

Chapter 14

Who Invited Your Dog to Dinner?

Having a child changes your life. Having a child when your career involves going out on tour and caring for twenty animals *really* changes your life.

I had never been fond of the road, and after Jenna was born in 1997, I really wanted to be at home to help raise her. I made a promise to Dorothy that I wouldn't take any tours or other jobs that required me to be away for more than a month. So, for the next three years I concentrated on more film and TV work—for example, we started handling the animals for *Sesame Street*—as well as setting up a new *Annie* tour. Dorothy, meanwhile, went back to the Bushnell Theater.

I also extended my relationship with the Humane Society of New York. I had been doing benefits for them for twenty years, and they had been my partners when I set up the "Stray Mutt" program for the twentieth-anniversary production of *Annie*. Now they asked if I would come in and make some suggestions to the staff to help them train some of New York's neediest pets. I was honored that they would ask me at all because I was just a show business trainer. After a few months, they hired me as a consultant and gave me the title director of animal behavior. I would go in once a week and set up training programs for problem dogs, as well as review intakes and adoptions. This is a post I still hold today.

Marion Seldes, as Carlotta Vance, with Noelle in *Dinner at Eight*. *Photo by Joan Marcus*

I was involved with two failed Broadway tryouts during this time. One was a musical based on the Danny Kaye movie musical *Hans Christian Andersen*—we opened and closed in San Francisco. The other was *Paper Doll*, a new play about the life and times of author Jacqueline Susann and her dog, Josephine. It starred Marlo Thomas and F. Murray Abraham and had tryouts in Pittsburgh, Raleigh, North Carolina, and New Haven, Connecticut.

In October 2002 I got a call from one of the original press agents from *Annie*, Barbara Carol. We had stayed in touch over the years, and she had always followed my career. Now she was the press agent for Lincoln Center. She called to say they were doing a revival of a George S. Kaufman play called *Dinner at Eight*, to be directed by the famous Gerald Gutierrez. The actress who would be handling the dog in the show was my old friend Dorothy Loudon, the original Miss Hannigan on Broadway. We hadn't worked together since *Annie 2* closed after tryouts in Washington, D.C.

By the end of the month I had arranged a deal, spent time with the director, and found out he wanted a Pekinese for the part. The dog was being carried in, so I felt that two weeks of rehearsal would be enough. I would then turn it over to a handler to run for the final eight weeks. My rehearsals started in early November. We would make it to the stage a week later, and the first performance was a week after that.

As soon as I got the first call, I immediately started looking for new dogs, using a great new tool. In the late 1990s, something wonderful happened to the animal adoption problem. Betsy and Jared Saul, a married couple, set up a website called Petfinder.com. They were able to attract corporate sponsors and take the site national. Today it's a search engine for pets. Shelters from all over the country list the animals they have available for adoption. On Petfinder.com you can search on the type of animal, breed, and gender and get a list of all matching animals close to where you live. It's probably one of the best uses of the Internet I know and a great tool for helping animals.

It's also a great time-saver for me. Now, instead of getting on the phone and calling animal shelters, I was able to go on the Internet, type in "Pekinese" and my zip code, and find all the Pekinese that were available for adoption in a hundred-mile radius. I found a small, five-year-old Pekinese named Noelle. She was a victim of a divorce and long working hours, meaning she was being left alone for long periods. Many nights she was tied out with another dog all night long. She was cute and just needed a little one-on-one attention.

She had been taken in by a group called Amanda Connection that did foster care in Newtown, Connecticut. When I called them and told them the situation, they were very happy to place her with me. Even though she got along with people, she wasn't that good with other dogs, but I said I would work on that and she probably would spend most of her time alone in New York City. When the show was over, we would find a good placement for her with the help of the humane group.

Three days after I located Noelle, I met her and adopted her. She had been shaved down because her coat was a mess, but she was healthy, personable, very calm, and very loving. After we cleaned her up, we brought her in. The director liked her and thought she would do well on the show, and we were set. Meanwhile, I was once again staying with Sarah Jessica Parker's family in New Jersey. Sarah has seven brothers and sisters, and even though they're all grown up, her parents still live in a big house with lots of bedrooms for when the kids and grandkids visit. Whenever I needed a place to stay, I was always welcomed as one of the family.

When I came into the rehearsal hall in Lincoln Center the first day, there, lying on the couch, was Dorothy Loudon. She saw me coming, stood up, extended her arms, and gave me a warm, welcoming hug. It was good to see her working again. She was a very talented actress, but at nearly seventy, there weren't a lot of roles for someone her age. She hugged me like I was a long-lost friend. She said, "Billy, it is so good to see you." It seemed to me like she held the hug a little longer than usual, as though she needed the support. I thought she was just happy to see an old friend, so I held on as long as she did. Then we sat down and talked.

The first thing she said to me was, "I'm so glad it's you, because when I got the part, I was afraid of working with a dog. You remember I'm afraid of dogs." It came back to me then that while we had worked together on *Annie*, she told me she hadn't grown up with dogs and felt uncomfortable around them. I'm sure she was worried some stranger would come in with an out-of-control dog, and she would have to deal with it. I told her immediately that I would do anything she needed in order to feel comfortable, and she was very grateful.

When it came time to go in and do our scene, we went into the rehearsal hall where I introduced Noelle to everybody. Gerry, the director, had his Yorkie, Edna, with him, his constant companion. At first I was surprised that there was a dog in the rehearsal room, since no one had mentioned it to me. When I asked the stage manager if we could ask Gerry to remove his dog, she said, "Oh no, oh no. The dog stays at every rehearsal. Gerry is never parted from that dog." Now, when I had adopted Noelle, they had told me she wasn't good with other dogs because she had only lived with one dog all her life. When I brought her to my farm, with our twenty other dogs, we made certain we didn't overwhelm her. We matched her up with dogs her own size and temperament so she wouldn't feel the need to protect herself. She had gotten along well with little dogs her own size in our home but bigger dogs scared her, and if a dog of any size barked at her, she immediately became defensive.

Well, after spending an hour or so sitting with Dorothy on the couch and letting Dorothy pet her and see how nice and calm she was, just as Noelle felt relaxed and we went into the rehearsal room, Edna started to bark. Of course, Noelle became agitated and barked back. This was going to be a problem. The whole time that Dorothy was trying to do her blocking, Edna would start barking, and then Noelle would bark and squirm. I didn't blame the dogs. Edna was used to being the only dog when she went to the theater with Gerry. She was fondled, she got treats—she was really the alpha dog of Gerry's theatrical world. Now here was an intruder in her space, so of course she would protect it and bark. Noelle, on the other hand, had been prepped to believe *she* was an alpha dog because we needed her to be courageous in front of an audience. She had been doing some preliminary training and getting lots of treats, so she was also protecting her space.

After the first day of rehearsal, I went up and spoke with Gerry, because once Noelle started barking, it unnerved Dorothy. It made her feel insecure about the dog and wonder if Noelle was going to bite her. I was afraid Noelle would unbalance Dorothy, since she already seemed a little frail and unsteady on her feet, and she was afraid she'd drop the dog. But when I asked Gerry if we could remove Edna from the room, he looked at me as if I had asked a really inappropriate question. He said, "No, of course not. You just have to train that dog to ignore Edna."

While I appreciated his devotion to his dog, I didn't understand why he would let his personal feelings get in the way of the show. We were only talking about having Edna go to someone's office while we did this one scene, and then she could return. But since he was a famous director, he could make demands and the producers would make sure those demands were met. In this situation, I had to make Noelle stop barking.

Now, if it had been another actress in another situation, an actress who liked dogs or was a little steadier on her feet, she would have been able to say to Noelle, "No—stop that," and Noelle would have stopped. Unfortunately, Dorothy didn't feel she could do that. I kept stepping in and interrupting the action to make the dog stop barking, even though she was generally just responding to Edna. But however we did it, I was able to reassure Dorothy that once we got onstage, Edna wouldn't be around, Noelle would calm right down, and I'd be there to help her get through it. She would always hug me and thank me for my kindness and for helping her.

I tried to keep an eye on Dorothy that week. I'd go out and get her lunch. Sometimes I'd see her sitting by herself, so I'd sit down and talk with her. We would reminisce about old times, and she would tell me wonderful stories about her career. It was fun just sitting with her and hearing about the theater. At the end of the week, we moved upstairs into the Vivian Beaumont Theater in Lincoln Center to begin tech rehearsals. The set was a rich apartment in New York City, and there was a stairway in the middle of the stage that went down into the basement, which is where the dressing rooms were. When people entered the apartment, they either entered through the front door or they came up the stairs, as if they were coming from another floor in the apartment. Dorothy's first entrance was up these steps.

These were the first rehearsals using the sets, costumes, and lights. Tech rehearsals are very painstaking; you go from cue to cue, from beginning to end. By the end of the first day, we had just made it up to Dorothy's entrance. I had heard the cues coming, and I went over to her dressing room to meet her and walk with her to where she would make her entrance. She needed to navigate three steps to get there, and when we reached them, she turned to me and said, "Billy, give me a hand." I extended my arm and she held on and she had quite a bit of difficulty getting up those three steps.

It alarmed me. Dorothy was acting like a much older person. She put so much pressure on my arm that I was concerned she might fall. When she looked up at the full flight of stairs that would take her to the stage, she said, "I can't do it." At that point I ran to get the stage manager and her dresser. The stage manager said they had someone there to assist her, but it didn't help. She was already uncertain about holding on to Noelle, and now she had to climb these stairs. Dorothy panicked. She finally made her way up the stairs for her first entrance with the help of her dresser and the stage manager. When she got onstage, Edna started barking from the audience where she was sitting with Gerry. Then Noelle started barking. I had to go onstage to calm Noelle down.

Dorothy was worried. But what concerned me was that she couldn't make it up the stairs without assistance. I was worried about the safety of my old friend. When I spoke to her about it later, she assured me she'd be fine as long as someone was there to help her. But as rehearsals continued over the next two days, it was obvious she was having more and more trouble. On the third day she actually fell and twisted her leg. It was becoming apparent to everyone that she wouldn't be able to do the show. The producers started calling around to find a replacement.

Dorothy missed the Saturday rehearsal. It was heartbreaking to see this once-vibrant, award-winning actress undone by a flight of stairs. Her brilliant performance wasn't going to be seen because she couldn't make her entrance. Sadly, we soon found out why Dorothy had such a hard time. She was suffering from cancer and died within a year. I will always remember her as Miss Hannigan—a multitalented triple threat and a true Broadway star.

On Sunday, five days before our first performance, we were called together and told that Marian Seldes would be replacing Dorothy Loudon. Marian is one of America's most accomplished stage actresses and someone I admire a great deal. She had actually done a stint in *Annie 2*, playing alongside Dorothy, and then in the revised *Annie Warbucks* at Goodspeed, so I knew she was comfortable working with animals. I had actually thrown a small party for her when she eloped with Garson Kanin during the run of *Annie Warbucks*—she had never forgotten and to this day she always gives me a big hug when she sees me. We were fortunate to have such an actress who could come in, learn the part, and deal with dogs.

The first day of rehearsal, Noelle and Edna started barking at each other as soon as Noelle came out onstage. When the scene was finished, Marian came offstage and asked, "Why was the dog barking?" I explained about Edna and how Gerry wouldn't be parted from her. She said, "Oh, okay." In the final scene of the play when Noelle came in, the same thing happened. She was barking uncontrollably. We stopped for a second and Marian said, "Bill, what can we do to get this dog to stop barking?" I said, "I don't know how to say this, but I've asked the director for two weeks now if he would remove his dog, and I've been told by the producers, the management, even Gerry himself, that he is never parted from this dog."

She smiled with her glorious smile, turned toward the audience, and said, "Gerry?"

"Yes?" he said.

"Could you remove Edna from the theater? She's disturbing Noelle."

Good things come in small packages.

And Gerry, much to everyone's surprise, said, "Anything for you, Marian—anything for you." At which point his assistant came and took Edna out of the theater.

I was dumbfounded. Neither the producers, nor the stage managers, nor any of the actors had been able to convince Gerry to remove his dog, and here was Marian Seldes, in a very polite, public way, asking him to do it—and he did. It wasn't until after the rehearsal was over that I asked Marian how she'd accomplished it. She smiled and said, "Oh, darling, I was his college professor. Apparently he still listens to me." We had a good laugh, and for the last four days before the first performance, Noelle was able to get used to the stage, be quiet, get treats, and appear with one of the great ladies of the American theater.

The play opened in mid-December. I did the first week of performances and got Noelle settled in while Ryan Gaffney, my new trainer, followed me around. Ryan was the brother of Lauren Gaffney, who had played Annie in *Annie Warbucks*. One of the best things about my job is that I have gotten to work with so many wonderful young people and, really, become part of their extended family. Ryan was a young filmmaker between projects. He was able to come in, run the show, and make a guaranteed salary for eight weeks. At the end of the run, I had another good New York credit—and Ryan had a new dog. He and his girlfriend had fallen in love with Noelle and asked if they could keep her. She's been living happily with them ever since.

Chapter 15

You Gotta Have a Gimmick

Gypsy is one of the best Broadway shows ever written, with a book by Arthur Laurents, music by Jule Styne, lyrics by Stephen Sondheim, and original choreography by Jerome Robbins. Based on the life story of Gypsy Rose Lee, her sister "Baby" June, and her mother Rose, it tells the backstage story of the life of kids in show business. It is brilliant in so many ways.

I was connected to this story in a very special way. The last actress to play Miss Hannigan on Broadway was June Havoc, Gypsy Rose Lee's sister. In the early 1980s she was in her mid-sixties, but she could still sing, dance, and tell a joke like no one's business. Coming into the company of any established show is hard, but I had heard that she was an animal lover. So on her opening night there was a knock on her door, and when she opened it, Sandy was sitting there with a rose in his mouth and an opening-night note. I couldn't have given her anything better.

June didn't just like animals, she loved them. The stories of her family adopting stray animals were all true, and throughout her life, June has rescued thousands of animals to her farm in Connecticut. We have been friends for more than twenty-five years. Contrary to popular belief, she and Gypsy were close during the last part of Gypsy's life, and June has some of Gypsy's cherished belongings. When I visited, June would show me Gypsy's striptease

Michael McCormick, as Uncle Jocko, and Bernadette Peters, as Rose, with Coco in *Gypsy*.
Photo by Joan Marcus

costumes, photographs, and other memorabilia. I remember opening what I thought was a script and seeing the first draft of Gypsy's memoirs, which she had typed herself. June told me that the memoirs and the musical based on them had been fictionalized, and that it didn't happen that way.

Gypsy has been revived frequently. Angela Lansbury did a Broadway production in 1974, and Tyne Daly won the Tony Award for her performance as Mama Rose in 1989. I was asked to work on the 1989 production, but the producers refused to hire one of my trainers. In the show there are a small dog and a lamb. When you have an infant or very young animal, you need to provide special care and supervision. Instead of paying for my trainer to provide that care, they decided to hire one of the actresses in the show to take care of the animals. They also hired one of my competitors to deliver lambs to the theater whenever they were needed.

This poor actress had to learn—on her feet—how to take care of lambs. When that particular show was on tour in Hartford, I got a call from the local theater manager saying the lamb was very sick and asking whether I knew any vets in the area who would take care of it. I wondered why they would call me. Why should I help my competitors? But I had to help because an animal's life was in peril. I gave them my vet's home number, and they saved its life.

In November 2002 I was contacted about a new revival, one that would star the fabulous Bernadette Peters. This gave me another strong connection to the show. Besides being one of the great ladies of Broadway, Bernadette is also an animal lover. In 1996, in an effort to bring all the New York City animal shelters together, she partnered with Mary Tyler Moore to create a one-day event called Broadway Barks. Each year in August, all the New York animal shelters come and set up tables in Shubert Alley and bring animals for adoption. They are brought up onstage and introduced by Broadway stars. I had helped Broadway Barks from the very beginning, either in my role with the Humane Society of New York or by bringing my rescued animal stars to participate in the event. In 2005 Bernadette honored my work with an award. It means a lot to me that my Broadway peers who love animals recognized the work that I do. I'm sure that when Bernadette agreed to do *Gypsy*, she suggested that I work on it. Rehearsals would begin in January 2003, with the first performance at the end of March and the official opening night in May.

Since this was a revival of an older show, the animals were just props. I actually knew stagehands who worked on the original production with Ethel Merman. They told me some pretty scary stories of the tryouts in Philadelphia. In the original script, as in real life, the characters had a monkey. During the tryouts, the monkey destroyed the set and ultimately was cut. When she was a child, Gypsy Rose Lee got a lamb on her birthday, and in the show, she sings a lullaby to it. The stagehands told me that they bought the lambs from the meat market. Lambs grow very fast, so when they got too big to be carried onstage, they had a barbecue.

The lambs, in particular, worried me. I thought the little dog would be easy—in the photos that I had seen of the other productions, they had used Yorkshire terriers. June said, though, that they owned all kinds of mutts when they were growing up. But taking care of an infant lamb is very intense. It involves bottle-feeding every four to six hours, diaper changes, and exercise. Plus, it is illegal to house farm animals in New York City apartments. I had gotten away with it with the pig in *Alice in Wonderland*, but this was going to be a very high-profile show.

I needed to find someone with a truly nurturing personality, who was animal savvy, showbiz savvy, and crazy enough to take this on. Then I remembered another great animal lover from my past. Marge Merklinghaus is the mother of Shelley Bruce, the second Broadway Annie. Marge is a stage mother in the best sense of that term—smart, protective, and dedicated to caring for kids. She had always had small dogs from the time I first met her, and she had become an avid wildlife rescuer. She lived by the shore in southern New Jersey, where she rescued ducks and geese and all sorts of other birds. She always had dogs and parrots in her house. Some years back I needed geese for a film, so I called Marge. She brought in some geese, and we had a ball on the set, laughing and remembering old times. Jokingly, she had said if you ever get a show, call me—so now I did.

At first Marge laughed, because she was retired, and said "I don't know anything about sheep." But I had seen her with plenty of human babies, and I knew that she could handle it. I was worried about the commute from South Jersey, because it was an hour and a half each way, but she was up for it. She had more energy than I did.

The show was being directed by Oscar Award–winning director Sam Mendes. I really wanted to rescue a dog for this show, but Sam wasn't sure what kind of dog he wanted, and I couldn't just pull dogs out of a shelter for him to look at. We weren't really able to pin him down about the breed. He said he wanted a dog between 10 and 12 pounds, so I sent a picture of Noelle the Pekinese, who was just closing from her run in *Dinner at Eight*. She was about 12 pounds, but he couldn't make up his mind.

The first day of rehearsal they have what's called a "Meet and Greet," usually in the morning—everyone says hello, the producers and creative team introduce themselves, there's coffee and donuts. In the afternoon is the first read-through of the script. I saw Bernadette and she gave me a big warm hug. We smiled and chatted and she whispered in my ear, "Remember, I'm allergic to dogs." I laughed and said, "Oh, come on, you're joking, right?" She got very serious, looked me in the eye, and said, "No, seriously. I'm allergic to certain dogs, so we have to rescue one that I can work with." Then she hugged me and walked away. I was in shock. I had planned on getting a small rescue dog, but now we needed a hypoallergenic dog, and a pound search wouldn't work. I immediately pulled over our stage managers and our producers, and they were incredulous. How could one of New York City's biggest animal lovers be allergic to dogs? She had two dogs— but it turns out they were dogs she learned she could tolerate.

I wanted to make sure that I found the right dog for Bernadette because I didn't want to be responsible for causing her any vocal problems. I said to the producers, "Let's set up a test in two days. I'll bring in a bunch of dogs and let's see how she reacts." I had Noelle the Pekinese, and I found two Yorkies and a Yorkie mix. Bernadette had an allergic reaction to them. Marge was with me, and she went everywhere with her teacup poodle, Peanut, who was all black and about five years old and she weighed all of 5 pounds. Bernadette saw her peeking out of her bag, picked her up, kissed her, and said, "This is the dog I want." The problem was, Peanut was so small and all black. She looked like a big fluff ball. Sam Mendes turned to me and said, "Get one of these, but make it look like a Yorkie."

This was becoming a huge problem. We had budgeted to adopt a dog from a local shelter, not create a nationwide search. We went on the Internet but didn't find any parti-colored teacup poodles, which have coloring like a Yorkie. We did find a few breeders throughout the country, but they were asking $1,000 to $2,000 per puppy. We would have to fly out and see them if we were going to spend that much money. All of this was going to run up a big bill. The managers were getting angry at us, but we had to remind them we were just trying to meet the requirements of the director and the star.

After weeks of searching, we finally heard through some contacts that there was a six-month-old female parti-colored poodle living in an old shed in someone's backyard in Alabama, and they would sell it for $600. We contacted the owner. Marge did her best to make friends and made plans to fly down to see the dog. The day before she was to fly, they called and said the dog was sick and at the vet's. Two days later, after hospitalization for a cold, the price was $800. As Marge planned to go down again, they called and said the dog had almost died. Marge now was so worried that she finally drove to Alabama to get the dog.

Marge refused to tell me the whole story of what she found there because she said the conditions were so bad. Five days later she got this little girl back to New York and decided to call her Coco Chanel. She brought her into rehearsal where she met Bernadette, and they fell instantly in love. But Coco was going to require months of special care. Luckily, Marge was an expert on these little teacup breeds—Coco weighed three and a half pounds when we got her but blossomed in Marge's care.

While Marge was working on the dog, I tackled the sheep problem. I had what seemed like a simple choice—I could wait until spring and buy a dwarf lamb that would stay small enough for the role, or I could go to the

meat market, where they would have lambs bred for slaughter. For a moment I envisioned my backyard filled with sheep, because the only reason anyone would take these lambs once they got older would be to eat them, and I couldn't have that!

I called an old friend, an animal rescue photographer named Mary Bloom. She had worked at the American Society for the Prevention of Cruelty to Animals as an exotic animal consultant, and whenever I needed advice about exotic animals, I called Mary. When I got in touch this time, she laughed and told me of a wonderful secret two hours from my home—an organic sheep farm. It was run by a wealthy man who created gourmet organic sheep milk and cheese on pristine lands. He produced them year-round, and in order to do that he had to have pregnant sheep year-round.

This farm was in the New England hills. It was almost too good to be true. I called and explained the situation to the farm manger. He laughed at the prospect and invited me up for a tour. The farm was a dream. The sheep were free range and had beautiful barns. The nursery was clean and had fifty lambs at a time year-round. We agreed that I would pay them $100 per lamb, and they said they would gladly take the sheep back when they were too big to be carried onstage. It all seemed too good to be true because I could go back and tell Bernadette Peters and the producers (and the world!) that the lambs came from a beautiful farm and returned to live their lives in peace as milking sheep. I brought home the first baby lamb. My daughter, Jenna, loved naming things. The hundreds of stuffed toys she owned all had names. She took one look at the baby and decided to call her Violet.

We finally had our hypoallergenic dog and our lambs. Because the animals were just carried onstage, we waited until the cast and crew were in the theater in tech rehearsals before we brought them in. I had been promised they would build a dressing room for us, four walls and a door where the animals would be safe and out of the way. When we arrived, I was upset. The room wasn't built—we had two dogs in a crate, a crying lamb, and no place to sit. I ran into the production manager, who had been the head carpenter on the original production of *Annie,* and he remembered us. When he heard that we had no room, he said, "Don't worry, Billy, it'll be there for you tomorrow." You know you've made it on Broadway when the stagehands take care of you.

The next day when we arrived we had a small but great room with a door. As we started working onstage with Sam Mendes, there were a million things going on with the sets, lighting, and costumes. We were coming in six days before the first performance. Everybody knew what was going on except for us. The first time that I walked up onstage with the baby lamb, Sam Mendes turned to me and said, "How are you going to stop it from going to the bathroom onstage?"

"Daddy, this is the best show-and-tell ever."

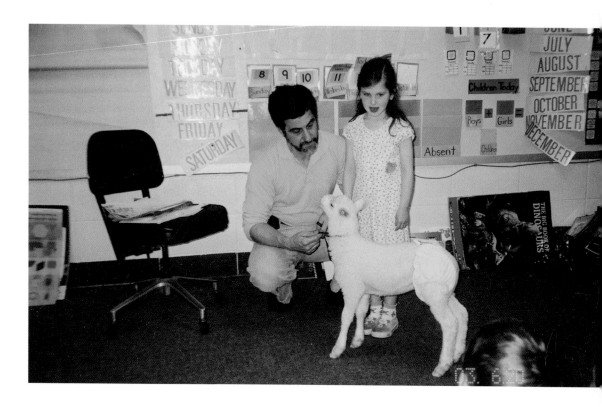

"Well, we'll need to put a diaper on her."

"I'd prefer it if we didn't," he said.

"If we had a seven-day-old human baby onstage, there'd be no way to prevent it from going to the bathroom. The same applies to this lamb," I said. So he agreed to allow us to create a costume, a cloth diaper that went over the Pampers that we used.

Coco's part was simple—she would be carried in with Bernadette as she made her entrance through the house and then get passed around onstage to the actors. The lamb was carried on and had to be quiet for an entire number. Bernadette was a pro and needed no help handling dogs. The plum role of Gypsy Rose Lee went to a young actress by the name of Tammy Blanchard. She was very sweet and very hardworking but unfamiliar with animals. Violet, our first baby lamb, had already bonded with Marge and me. We would feed her right before she went on to quiet her, but it didn't help. She'd look offstage and cry for us. We taught Tammy a holding method to keep Violet tight against her body, and that helped quiet her down. Finally, she learned not to struggle. She'd still cry for us a little, but for the most part, we had worked out all the bugs.

The first performance went well. I slept on Marge's couch until a day after the first performance, and then I had to leave to go to an out-of-town performance of *Paper Doll*, which was having its pre-Broadway tryout in New Haven, Connecticut. In two weeks, Violet went from 7 pounds to 14. She was doubling in size weekly. The breed that's used for milking comes from Iceland, and they grow very large. I had to run up and get our second lamb—Jenna named her Daisy. She decided to start a flower theme for all the lambs. In mid-April, Daisy went into the show and Violet came back with me to our house and then back to the farm. When I first put her back in the nursery, all white and clean and smelling of baby powder, she really stuck out. But within minutes she was running around and playing with the other lambs.

The drama of acquiring and handling the animals was nothing compared to the drama of the negotiations on this show. The producers claimed they hadn't budgeted for the animals. My deal was that they had to pay the costs of acquiring and transporting the animals, as well as the cost of the handler and my fee. Together, my trainer's salary and my fee equaled the amount of one chorus person's salary. It often happens that we have to start work before our contracts are signed, and that was the case with this production. Once Marge started working, they paid for her time, but they kept changing the terms of my contract, and I wouldn't agree to them after we had started working. Without a contract, they wouldn't pay me. I refused to give up on the things I had agreed to, and soon it became a stalemate.

As the weeks went by, I was at a crossroads. I hired one of the best entertainment lawyers to represent me, but nothing was resolved. After eight weeks of my animals showing up and doing a Broadway show without pay, I had had it. I took a stand. I was going to leave on my terms rather than stay on theirs. I spoke to Marge about it, and she was behind me 100 percent in my decision to leave the show.

In passing, Marge told Bernadette Peters the animals would be leaving. When Bernadette learned I hadn't been paid, she picked up the phone in her dressing room and called the managers and told them to fix it. Bernadette was adamant that Marge, the animals, and I were going nowhere. Within two days my contract was signed on my original terms—but it took an animal-loving star to help us out. No one has ever stood up for us the way that Bernadette Peters did.

The show got great reviews and ran for a year. Bernadette received another Tony Award nomination. We went through twenty-three lambs; Jenna named them all after flowers except one dwarf lamb that we found, named Jack. He would have lasted longer but he started growing horns. Marge put bows on them, but by the end he started hurting people. Marge and Coco had become inseparable, and I decided that she should take Coco home. Marge was sad to see the lambs go. We had become experts on lamb diet and behavior.

When I remember *Gypsy*, I remember two great ladies, June Havoc and Bernadette Peters, and how their love for animals continues to inspire me.

Chapter 16

Easy as Pi

In the fall of 2003 I found a message on my answering machine: "Hello. How much would it cost to have a dog in a show?" We get calls like this all the time. I thought it was probably some young theater student doing a college play, so I called her back. I politely explained that training a dog took weeks or months. "What does the dog have to do?" I asked. She replied, "All the dog has to do is run onstage and lick an actor. We were thinking of a Dalmatian."

I thought to myself, This will never happen. I explained that Dalmatians were very high-strung dogs and that I didn't have one currently, so I would have to start from scratch. The cost would be thousands of dollars. I was certain that would end her interest, but I asked why she wanted the dog. After a pause she said, "Well, I'm Tara Young, Susan Stroman's assistant. Susan has been asked to create a new American ballet for the New York City Ballet to celebrate the Balanchine Centennial." I couldn't believe my ears. Susan Stroman was Broadway's hottest director. The New York City Ballet is one of the world's leading dance companies. Balanchine was a genius. And I was trying to lose the job!

Stroman already had a reputation as a brilliant choreographer, but she had taken Broadway by storm, directing and choreographing the musical

Tom Gold, as The Boy, with Pi in *Double Feature*. *Photo by Paul Kolnik*

version of Mel Brooks's *The Producers*. It had opened on Broadway and won more Tony Awards than any show in Broadway history. Plus, she was known as one of the nicest people to work with, down-to-earth but demanding excellence.

Tara explained that Susan's concept for the ballet was based on silent movies. The costumes and sets would be black-and-white, which is why they wanted a black-and-white dog. I had to rescue this situation somehow, so, feeling like an idiot, I sheepishly said, "I don't have a Dalmatian, but I have a black-and-white Boston terrier. Can I e-mail you a picture?" She said, "Oh, absolutely." After I took down the e-mail address, I said, "And because this dog is already trained and we own it, it would save you a substantial amount of money." After I told Dorothy what had happened, she said, "See, I told you Pi would work."

I did have my doubts about Pi. In 2001, he had been turned over to the Boston Terrier Rescue Group of New York. He had been too rambunctious for the family that owned him, so they had left him tied outside to a tree for months. The rescue group had socialized him and given him basic obedience training, even agility training. By summer 2002, he was ready for adoption. That summer, Jenna had started asking for a dog of her own. I argued that she could pick any of the dogs we already owned, but Dorothy said it wouldn't be the same. I argued that Jenna was too young, but Dorothy knew better. Before I knew it, Pi was coming to the house for a visit.

When we met Pi, he was a handsome, confident, tough terrier, well trained but easily overstimulated—completely wrong for our household and a five-year-old girl. He was eyeing the horses and the llamas and barking at all the other dogs. I said I didn't think he would fit in. Jenna gave me the eyes. Dorothy gave me the smile. Pi sat on our picnic table and paid no attention to me at all. I envisioned him tied to that tree, alone and afraid of people. Then I thought about how far he had come. I decided he deserved a chance.

Now, Pi knew many commands, and he listened very well in a working session. And he did work for me—he was featured in a book about yoga called *Doga*, for which I provided the dogs. But he also chased the cats, chased the horses, and barked at the other dogs. He had food allergies and stomach problems. All in all, he had been more work than ten dogs put together. So I said to Dorothy, "You're crazy! He'll be chasing ballerinas all over that stage. I was just buying us time until we could find the right dog." We sent his picture anyway the next day and I got a call that afternoon. "Hello, is Bill there? This is Susan Stroman."

I almost fainted. She was warm and pleasant and loved the picture of Pi's face. In fact, her assistant director, Scott Bishop, had already made it his screensaver on the computer. She said, "Bill, I know nothing about dogs. What can we expect him to do?" I offered to come into New York to show her in person. I was floored—Pi and I were going to have a private session with Susan Stroman! On the appointed day I arrived at her New York penthouse and was greeted by Scott, her assistant director, and Tara, Susan's assistant choreographer. They screamed when they saw Pi, and he proceeded to jump all over them, much to my dismay. I was led into an all-white studio with mirrors, where I met Susan. She extended her hand with a warm and welcoming smile and said, "What a pleasure it is to meet you." I'm thinking, *a pleasure to meet me?* I was snapped back to reality by Pi attacking his reflection in a floor-to-ceiling mirror. Everybody was laughing, but I was so embarrassed.

They sat down and I went into my presentation. I showed them basic obedience, how Pi walked, sat, stayed, and came on command, all to hand signals. Pi was flawless. Then for the closing, I held a treat at shoulder height and Pi leapt straight up, spinning like an athlete, and that was it. Susan was so impressed she asked if he could do that onstage. I assured her that if he was going to do one thing, it would be jump around onstage.

She explained that the piece was called *Double Feature*. It would consist of two one-act ballets based on silent films. The second act was a comedy

Every star has an entourage.

called *Makin' Whoopee*, based on a Buster Keaton film. The basic story is boy meets girl. Girl has dog. Boy loses girl. Dog harasses boy. Boy gets girl in the end. She wanted a dog to do two or three quick comedic bits onstage and run off. As we brainstormed, she came up with her idea for the opening—the boy enters with a box of chocolates and the dog tries to steal them. In the next bit, the boy closes his eyes for a kiss from the girl, the girl walks off, and the dog kisses the boy. Later on, the boy is chased by a bunch of people—could the dog chase the boy as well? Wouldn't it be funny if the dog grabs the boy's pants leg? While Pi was trying to climb all over the furniture, I told Susan I thought we could get Pi to do most of the things she was asking. But I was a little leery of the chasing and biting part because he really loved to do that in real life.

She then explained the schedule. We would get the ballet company for one week of rehearsal, three days of tech rehearsals, and then seven performances. To accommodate that, she would create the ballet with her own dancers throughout the fall in bits and pieces, and then she would teach it to the ballet company. I explained that the lack of time would make it difficult for me to bond Pi with the dancer playing the boy, but I said if she was willing to try, I thought we could make it work.

But, again, I felt compelled to tell her the truth—Pi was a high-strung dog, and with his history, I wasn't sure if he would be right for the part. She asked me, "What does your gut tell you?" I said my instinct was that he was a survivor, and that if we could teach him the right things, he would have a chance to do it. She said to me, "Then if you're willing to try, so am I." I have never felt such a sense of support, respect, and collaboration as I did at that moment.

We began working one day a week, every two weeks, in a rehearsal room in Times Square. When I arrived, it was Susan, her assistant choreographer Tara, her assistant director Scott, and two of her dancers, Joanne Manning and Fergus Logan. We started the first cue, where Pi walks in with the girl and the boy comes onstage with chocolates. He takes one out and the dog leaps to try and steal it. He would jump three times and then the boy would take the treat and throw it offstage.

We gave Fergus a treat—Pi jumped and jumped and jumped. Susan was laughing. On cue Fergus threw it toward me and Pi chased it. The first time was great, so we tried it again. This time Pi didn't see the treat being thrown. So when Fergus turned around and put his hands on his hips, Pi thought he still had the treat in his hand and jumped up and nipped his side. *Oh my lord*, I thought, *my career's over*. Fortunately there was no blood, just a good pinch. We worked for about an hour to refine the trick. Susan was thrilled, but I had ten more gray hairs.

Two weeks later we had our next session. We ran that first part and Pi remembered it perfectly. During this session, we were going to work on the scene where he comes onstage and "kisses" the boy. Now, the old dog trainer's trick is to put peanut butter on someone's face where the audience can't see it. The first time we tried it, Pi saw the peanut butter and ran out to Fergus —the next thing I hear is "Owwww!" Pi had nipped his nose. The next time I tried putting the peanut butter closer to Fergus's ear, but Pi nipped it, too. Finally, I found a spot in the middle of Fergus's cheek and he got lots of kisses. Susan was happy. Fergus, who was being a real trouper, smiled. And I had twenty more gray hairs.

Week four was the scene where Pi had to run across the stage, chasing the boy—except I found out that Pi would be wearing a wedding dress and carrying a newspaper. "Okay," I said, "the dress we can do, but carrying things is not something terriers do." I gave Pi the rolled-up newspaper, and, of course, he immediately attacked it with glee. I wrestled it away from him and told Susan, "I'm going to have to work on this, but we can start practicing with the dress on and having him follow Fergus across the stage." For that rehearsal, we wrapped a piece of fabric around Pi's chest. Fergus had a treat and would run across the stage. When he got halfway, I'd release Pi. Fergus ran fast to avoid him. We also practiced the earlier bits and it seemed to go well.

On the break between weeks four and five, I practiced the retrieving with a tightly rolled newspaper. I would throw it, Pi would bring it back to me, and I had to give him a treat. Pi started to get the idea that the newspaper wasn't for chewing. We went in for week six, and I was able to show Susan that at least he wasn't shredding it. But our last bit was grabbing the boy's pant leg. This week I spared poor Fergus and showed Susan how I intended to make it happen. I took Pi's favorite toy and taped it to the inside of my pant leg. As he ran toward me, I knew what was coming—he missed the toy and got my leg. I was afraid that's exactly what would happen onstage. We started to brainstorm some other ways to get the same effect. Susan suggested maybe the sleeve of a jacket, but I still felt it was too close to the body.

As we were thinking, I suggested a hat, which could be held away from the dancer. Susan asked me to demonstrate, so I put the toy in a rag and Pi grabbed onto it. As far as he was concerned, he was playing tug-of-war with me. While he was doing that, I couldn't hear what Susan was saying, so I walked over to her while he was holding onto it, dragging him along behind me. She burst out laughing and that was it. In the four sessions where we had collaborated, we had come up with some pretty impressive behaviors, with complete success. She was ready to tell the New York City Ballet that it could be done, and she asked me again if I was still willing to do it. For her, I said, "anything."

A week later Susan called me—she had returned from a production meeting. The show was scenically larger than anything the New York City Ballet was used to, and there were concerns. Halfway through the meeting, she proudly told them that she had worked with me to create a whole choreographic part for a dog. Susan then told me they were adamant—there had never been a dog in the ballet, and they were already over budget and they would not approve it.

She said, "Bill, I'm afraid the New York City Ballet will not pay you to do *Double Feature*." Although I was disappointed I wouldn't be able to work with her, I thanked her for her support and her kindness. She replied, "They won't pay your fee, so I will."

I was speechless. No director should have to pay out of her own pocket for elements of a show she's creating. I said, "I should be paying *you* for the opportunity to be in this project." She said that Pi's performance was an important part of her vision, and it was her choice. I was a professional, she thought I should be compensated like one, and she wanted to do it. Now that's a sign of pure class. I could only agree.

We continued with our every-other-week rehearsals, and in December 2004, we had the real boy come in, principal dancer Tom Gold. He was a well-respected member of the company, but best of all, he was a dog lover. He had heard such wonderful things from Susan that he couldn't wait to work with us. Tom immediately got how easily Pi could be overstimulated, and they came together perfectly under Susan's direction. We had to take a break because the ballet company went into their Christmas schedule, so we didn't see Tom or the company until February 2004.

On Broadway, rehearsing, teching, and putting a show up on its feet is usually a four- to eight-week process. Here, Susan had three days. On the first day, there would be rehearsal in the New York City Ballet room with the entire company. The next day was the one chance we'd have to put the whole production together onstage. The first performance was the day after that. But these were experienced dancers—they could watch Susan's choreography and do it almost immediately.

I almost didn't make it to the first rehearsal. When I arrived at the New York City Ballet that morning, security stopped me and wouldn't let me in. They kept saying, "Sorry, sir, no dogs allowed." I called Scott on my cell, and he came down to get us in. Even though he was assistant director and extremely busy, Scott volunteered to help me throughout the run.

My main concern was getting Pi used to the company of fifty dancers. I wanted to make sure Pi wouldn't get overexcited with all the dancers chasing him. My plan was to have a speech for the company, tell them what the parameters were, and then start rehearsing. I walked into the room, put my bag down, took my coat off, and heard the ballet master say, "Quiet." I was introduced, and when I walked to the center of the room and turned to speak, it was like I was frozen in time. There I was in the middle of one of the world's most famous ballet troupes, surrounded by some of the world's most beautiful and talented dancers. For a moment, all I could do was marvel. The moment was broken when Pi started barking at all the girls. That made everyone laugh and released the tension in the room, allowing me to give my speech.

The first couple of times we ran the scene, Pi thought it was a free-for-all and chased everybody around the room. By the third time, he was locked in on me and he did it properly. He was flawless after that with Tom. We did the other behaviors, and it showed me that he would listen to Tom in any space where we would do this routine. The next day of rehearsal was onstage. I remember walking Pi onto the stage at the New York State Theater. I hadn't been on that stage in twenty-four years, since Richard Burton was there with *Camelot*. Pi couldn't have cared less about the space—he was ready to go to work. The lights and the scenery were no problem. I asked where my dressing room was, and the production manager said there were no rooms available. It seemed silly, they knew we were coming, but no provisions were made. The ballet still wasn't happy I was there.

I called Susan and Scott backstage. The production manager said I could wait in the loading dock, a large unheated space with a garage door that separated it from the street. I turned to Susan and said, "Pi would fall apart in this space." Getting annoyed that she was wasting time, Susan left and spoke to someone. At last I was led to a storage closet in the basement of the theater. It was an 8-foot-wide room with shelves on either side and no speaker for me to hear the show. There wasn't even a chair or heat. When I asked how I was going to hear my cues, Scott interrupted and said he would come down to get me at the appropriate times. Not the warmest reception for my work, but I was there for Susan, not for the ballet.

Susan had picked music by Irving Berlin for the first act and by Walter Donaldson for the second. It had to be reorchestrated because unlike Broadway, where there are twenty to twenty-five musicians in the pit, the New York City Ballet has a seventy-six-piece orchestra. It was stunning to listen to. Pi had a hard time ignoring them, but Tom kept him on track. We made it through the costumes, the lights, and even through the timpani. The last thing I had to worry about was the audience. This was a highly anticipated event, for both the ballet world and the Broadway world. The run had already sold out.

On opening night, Pi came out and did his first jumping cue, unaware of the audience. I was thrilled. His second cue was the kissing bit. He ran out to kiss Tom, but when the audience saw him and laughed, Pi turned with this look of wonderment, and I thought he was going to leap over the orchestra pit. At that moment the lights went to black and Tom tapped him on the butt and he followed Tom offstage. That was a close call. The third cue was when he chased Tom across the stage in his dress with the newspaper in his mouth. Now, imagine the opening-night audience for the New York City Ballet's celebration of Balanchine's centennial seeing a dog in a wedding dress running across the stage. This time, the laughter was huge. So huge that Pi stopped three feet away from where I waited in the wings and turned to the audience. I called to him, but he couldn't hear me over the applause. As I looked past him, I saw thirty-five dancers running toward us. I did what anyone would do at that moment. I reached out from the wings and grabbed him and dragged him to safety—which got an even bigger laugh. In fact, one of the reviews talked about the hands that came out and pulled the dog offstage. It was like some old vaudeville bit.

By the end Pi was so excited with what he had done, all he wanted to do was run and grab and chew something up, which is exactly what he did with Tom's hat. Pi went out and did that cue as the curtain came down to thunderous applause. We had made it through with no nips and no accidents, in spite of the fact that the ballet company didn't want us there. At the end Susan was so gracious. She thanked me for everything I had done, and I could only feel privileged to have worked with her. The show was a huge success. The dance review in the *New York Times* mentioned Pi: "There are two showstoppers. One is a routine by a Boston terrier." Later in that review, they talked about Tom Gold's star performance and they said, "One can't give away the duet with the Boston terrier." The ballet world had a new star—much to their dismay.

We did the run and once a ballet is created, it cannot be changed. One year later, the New York City Ballet did *Double Feature* again in their repertory, and this time they had to hire me. Of course, we still got the storage closet as a dressing room. It continues to run every other year and is a huge crowd pleaser. Scott comes to assist us backstage at every production. At the end of our second run, Susan came back and thanked me again. She said she was going to be directing the film version of *The Producers*, and she wanted Pi to be in it.

True to her word, I got a call from the props guy in the film, saying the director kept talking about this dog named Pi and if I knew where I could find him. Unfortunately, we were given the wrong time, so I arrived after the scene had been filmed. Susan found me, apologized, and promised to put Pi in another scene. The scene never made it to the film, but you can see it in the outtakes on the DVD.

Chapter 17

Chitty Chitty Bark Bark

In October 2003, during rehearsals for *Double Feature,* I received a call from a general management office I had never worked with before. They were representing a new musical called *Masada,* set in the Warsaw ghetto during the Nazi occupation. They needed two German shepherds as guard dogs. The manager mentioned they were also representing the Broadway transfer of the London musical hit, *Chitty Chitty Bang Bang.* Because it was a direct transfer, it would come to Broadway without an out-of-town tryout. They would need ten dogs to run onstage and jump on one actor, then run off. But that was next year. My first time with this management office and they were offering me one Broadway show, with the possibility of another! Not bad.

Masada never opened. In the meantime, I sent a proposal about getting the ten dogs for *Chitty Chitty Bang Bang.* In my proposal I explained that housing and transportation would be costly, but it could be done. Almost a year passed before I heard from the manager. I received an e-mail from him with more details from the London production. He said to save money, they would go with eight dogs. In the first act, four dogs would enter from each side of the stage, then jump on one actor in a number called "Toot Sweet." Two handlers in costume were onstage to gather up the dogs as the curtain fell and get them offstage. There was also a cross for

Ken Kantor, as Lord Scrumptious, with the cast and dogs in *Chitty Chitty Bang Bang*.
Photo by Joan Marcus

one dog about twenty minutes later, and we could go home when we were done. He wanted to know what the costs would be. He kept emphasizing that it was very simple, just one big trick, no more than twenty minutes. Economy was the key because this was such an expensive show.

I thought again about practical problems like housing and transportation. It's easy to find an apartment in New York with two dogs—but what landlord in his right mind would rent to someone with eight dogs? Even renting a house within driving distance of New York City would be problematic. Then there's transportation. We always drove our animals. Two dogs can fit into a cab or a car no problem, but we would need at least two vans and two handlers, each responsible for four dogs. The costs were rising fast. When the managers kept saying there were no special tricks, I explained that the dogs would need the same basic training whether they were onstage one minute or an hour—and housing, transportation, and trainer salaries would be the same, too. I also pointed out that on Broadway, my non-union handlers would not be allowed onstage, so the dogs would have to be controlled by Equity actors. My estimate of expenses was about $3,500 a week—without my fee. They said they would consider all the options and call me. In the meantime, I asked if I could meet the director to get more information. It just so happened he was coming to New York a week later, and a meeting was set up.

It was a very polite meeting. The director told me he had two sets of dogs in London and they alternated because it was so taxing on them. "They pretty much did whatever they wanted," he said. I said I would not allow that. The budget here only allowed for one set of dogs, and they would be trained for their own safety. He looked at me a little incredulously and said, "Can you do that?" I explained that I had been doing exactly that for twenty-five years, at which point he asked me what shows I had worked on. He had no idea who I was. He became very interested in my training ability and the idea that he might have more control over the dogs. When I asked what kinds of dogs he would like, he said, "I have a choice?" In London he had to take what he was given. He said he would like dogs, from very small to very large, that looked like they came from all parts of the English countryside. When I explained

I would need rehearsal time with the actors, since the handlers wouldn't be allowed onstage, he wasn't sure he could promise me that.

Then I said we needed an actor who was a dog lover. Unfortunately, he said he had already cast the role. My heart sank because I feared that they hadn't warned the actor about the dog stuff. Then he told me they were going to offer the role to an actor named Ken Kantor, and at that moment, I knew the show might work. Ken is a giant of a man, tall and very broad-shouldered. Dorothy had worked with him in summer stock when she was young, and I had done two shows with him. A fine actor and singer, he'd always loved dogs.

I was asked to come in two weeks before the first performance when the cast moved to the theater. Back when I was offered the job, I quickly started forming the dog group. My thoughts were to look for older, established breeds that you might have seen in Europe at the turn of the century. I decided we could get away with one mutt, and that could be a Sandy dog I had named Bard. The second dog we could use was Barney, my well-trained mini poodle. So I had my first two dogs, right in my backyard. Now I needed six more. The first dog I adopted without hesitation was Harriet, a pit bull from the Humane Society of New York. She could play the big, mean street dog. Also at the Humane Society, we had just gotten in a Cavalier King Charles spaniel puppy named Lady. She was better with dogs than with people, and I decided she could work.

I had become friends with Joanne Genelle, one of the actresses from the show *Paper Doll.* She was my age and ready to get out of performing. She and her husband had just moved to a house in upstate New York, and she had started volunteering on the board of a local animal shelter. She told me immediately of a two-year-old male beagle named Patches who, she said, was just a dream—sweet, easy to train, very loving. The other dog that came to her mind was a nine-year-old cocker spaniel who'd been dumped there because his owners went into a nursing home and no one in their family would take him in. His name was Sidney. I made an appointment to drive up and meet those two dogs. They both were very good and I adopted them.

In December 2004, the public relations firm called to say they wanted to do a dog audition for the press. I explained to them that many well-meaning pet owners would probably come and be very disappointed when their dogs couldn't be in the show. I told them the story of *Nick & Nora*—before I came on as trainer, they had a similar contest and ended up being sued for fraud when the owner found out his dog wouldn't actually be in the show. I also told them about *Alice in Wonderland* and the fake pig audition we'd set up and how successful that was. Unfortunately, the press office said they had to do this event, and they had to move forward. I politely refused to participate and said good luck. About a day later it hit me—I called them back and said, "I need two more dogs. How about we hold an open audition, but for shelter dogs only, and if there are any good dogs, I'll adopt them." "Brilliant," they said. The Hilton Theater made an arrangement with the Hilton Hotel to donate one of their ballrooms for the event. The press department promoted it with ten days' notice. Ken Kantor, my wife Dorothy, and I were the judges.

The hotel set up a small stage. Each shelter got to bring their contestant up, introduce themselves, and give the history of the dog. I then gave the dog a quick temperament test and talked to the judges. We had about thirty-five dogs, which we got down to ten. Then I had Ken meet these ten. I also had Bard, my Sandy dog, come up to meet them. The dogs that were not friendly with Bard left, and we were down to five.

What I thought was just going to be a big photo opportunity became a real-life drama. At that point we were going on almost two hours, which is very long for a press event, but not one camera left. Of the last five dogs, one had caught my eye immediately. He was a beautiful collie who looked just like my first dog, Rexie. I wanted a collie as an adult, but never got a show for one. This dog, named Argyle, was from Herding Dog Rescue of Long Island. His previous family gave him that name because he ate socks. After his second surgery as a puppy to remove socks, the family decided to keep him in the basement for the next seven months of his life. They finally agreed to release him to the rescue group. After hearing this story, I expected a shy, ten-month-old pup, but this dog jumped on me and started licking my face. He was doing exactly what he needed to do for the show with people cheering in a room full of cameras.

One of the other five dogs was named Fred. Abandoned as a small puppy, he had been raised at the American Society for the Prevention of Cruelty to Animals. They said he had housebreaking issues, but I could work on that. He also ran up to me and jumped all over me. The other three dogs were also good, so this was a hard decision to make. The moment came. I picked the dogs that had followed Bard and not challenged him, and the winners were Argyle and Fred. The room erupted with cheers, tears, and hugs. Quickly we got all the dogs onstage for a group photo. My dream of letting the world know shelter dogs are worthwhile was coming true. By the time the interviews were over, I was hoarse. It would take a couple of days before we got the dogs, but less than two months before the opening, I had our dogs.

"Argyle reminded me so much of my boyhood dog, Rexie."
Photo by David Handschuh/New York Daily News

In the weeks after this audition, news of it went all around the world. I got articles from as far away as South Africa and Japan. It had been a smashing success. Later, one producer congratulated me, saying the event had garnered over $250,000 in free advertising for the show. I was just glad it had focused on shelter dogs.

I began looking for a commercial space to live in, sort of an artist's loft. I knew of many cheap ones in Brooklyn. I was finding the places we could afford, though, were only in bad areas and not fit for man or beast. Then I stumbled upon a newly renovated storefront that had been an old plumbing garage. The owner put two beautiful wrought-iron doors on the front that you could drive a vehicle through, and put in new walls, new tiles, a beautiful kitchen, new heating, and air-conditioning. The basement was also renovated, and there was a bathroom downstairs and one upstairs. It was affordable, and fortunately, the owner loved dogs. At first I was afraid to take it, just in case the show closed, because it required a one-year lease. I would build a temporary bedroom on the first floor for the second trainer.

As for the transportation, vans were our regular mode of transportation or our small station wagon. The number of the dogs would mean two vans, and I thought that would just get too complicated. Dorothy found me a box truck for sale on the Internet. It was 12 feet long by 8 feet wide. I looked at it and knew I could build cages and make it work. The cost of that vehicle was $25,000. Between the lease and the truck, I wouldn't break even for one year—not a real good risk to take. Years ago, after my third flop, I decided to always break even by opening night. Dorothy and I talked about it, and we decided we should go for it. As we were in the final stretch getting ready for rehearsals, we started putting all the pieces together.

I lived at the apartment myself for the first two weeks. Spending that time alone with my new pack, away from the farm, really bonded us. I got to see who they were—who was timid, who was smart, who would train the best. Harriet, Bard, Barney, Argyle, and Fred trained very well. Patches, Lady, and Sidney took the longest to train. But in that month, they all started to come together.

The morning of our first rehearsal, we loaded up the dogs in our huge truck in Brooklyn and headed for New York City. When we got there we were supposed to have a street parking permit, but none had come in. Then I discovered our dressing room hadn't been built. With all the other technical issues, the crew hadn't gotten to it. I was very annoyed. I had eight dogs in New York City for their first trip and I couldn't unload them. I only had ten rehearsal days, and now I was going to lose one of those. I decided to leave. The dogs ended up spending four hours in the truck that day—they were a little jangled and very anxious to get back to their own apartment. After many calls to the office, I was promised the room would be ready for the next day.

When we arrived at noon, the stagehands were still plastering the walls and sweeping out the room—or perhaps "closet." Knowing we had eight dogs, they had built a 10-by-8-foot room with a single door—96 square feet for eight dogs and three people. I took a deep breath and we moved everybody in, but before I did, I told them to build one large shelf in the back so we could put cages underneath and have a space on top to sit. The cramped space put everybody on edge, humans and dogs. The dogs started to pick fights with each other. We kept Barney the poodle up on the shelf for the whole run of the play just so he wouldn't be trampled.

The cast and crew were naturally curious and would come to our door, but again the dogs would rush the door and then start fights to get people's attention. So for the first time ever, I had to impose a new rule: No visitors until further notice. That upset many people, but the conditions dictated it. The only exception was Ken Kantor, who needed to bond with the dogs.

The technical part of the show was so difficult and they were so behind schedule, no time was given to the dogs beyond the five-minute breaks when the actors and crew stepped away. We would hear the break, and we would run the dogs up to see the stage, but we never had quality time to really train them. This became the final sticking point in my negotiations with the managers. If I didn't get the time, I couldn't guarantee a performance, and they wouldn't guarantee the time. Four days after we arrived, we finally got to work onstage in the scene. We had the entire cast onstage, but the dogs were wound up like springs.

Fortunately, Ken Kantor had spent all his offstage time in our room. He'd come in, sit on the floor, and get smothered with hair and dog kisses. By only allowing Ken to come in, and Ken being so good with them, they bonded to him very quickly. But take eight friendly dogs and let them go on a stage full of actors, and they all went wild. The director actually loved it—but the issue to me was that the curtain, with a heavy lead pipe in the bottom, was coming down at the same moment to enclose them in an 8-foot space upstage. The director thought it would be funny if they ended up on the wrong side of the curtain, but I was concerned for their safety. I wanted them to stay with Ken

A four-legged
chorus line.
Photo by Sandra DeFeo

as he led them to an open pen waiting stage right.

We didn't get back to that scene for another four days, and again, the dogs found Ken, but then they scattered and were almost hit by the curtain. By dress rehearsal, after only three tries, the dogs did it. I was amazed at their work together. However, there was a second part to the scene. The stage had a "runway" that curved around between the orchestra pit and the audience. They wanted the first dog out of the pack to enter along this runway. I picked Barney to do it because he didn't like the other dogs and he had the most stage experience. But then the director said they wanted him to enter and exit downstage, close to the curtain. The set design had been altered from the London production, and my trainers were going to be upstage handling the other dogs. How could we be two places at once? Obviously, we couldn't, but the director said that was our problem. The company managers said the stage managers would help out, but the stage managers weren't pleased at all. Meanwhile, we had less than a week to teach Barney to do a difficult cross with perfect strangers. He learned it— but each time he failed, it could be traced back to the fact that he was being handled by people who didn't know how or when to release him.

Our first public preview came, and three of the dogs got distracted by the audience and ended up on the wrong side of the stage, scared and confused. I was furious. Being underprepared meant the dogs were almost injured, and I refused to put those three on until we got proper rehearsal. The managers insisted they were paying me for eight dogs. Continuing technical problems meant there was still no rehearsal time. As we got a chance to rehearse, we were able to get all the dogs back onstage. Again, that was basically because of Ken Kantor. He continued to volunteer to come in on his own time, even when the other actors weren't there.

But there were many other problems with the show. The publicity department had done a great job—but American audiences didn't really understand British humor. And the creative team resisted changing anything that had worked so well in London. I've always felt that *Chitty Chitty Bang Bang* was to the British public what *The Wizard of Oz* is to Americans. It's the familiar, beloved story they grew up with. While we here in America liked the 1968 film with Dick Van Dyke, we didn't relate to it in the same way.

The dogs and I continued doing publicity for the show. I spoke with pride about the fact that our dogs were rescued. Opening night came and the reviews were mixed, with good notices for the stage effects, our brilliant actors, and even the dogs, but less enthusiasm for the story and the show overall.

For the most part, the dogs stayed on track. Ken had his clothes shredded by jumping dogs, and he had to start wearing gloves to protect his fingers from little nips. The dogs all had their quirks. Harriet and Patches, the beagle, were always on mark and did it right every night. Fred had to go out every hour to relieve himself. Lady, the King Charles spaniel, would sneak in between all the other dogs' legs, grab the treats, and run. Argyle, the collie, just followed everybody around—until halfway through the run he was hit by the curtain, and after that he refused to go on, even though we kept trying. Bard just ran across the stage and wouldn't stop. Sidney, the cocker, would follow the group and bark and nip at everyone's heels.

Sidney never seemed interested in treats, and I really didn't understand why. Then it became clear. One night, Patches bumped into Sidney, pointing him toward the orchestra pit. I happened to be in the audience, and I watched in horror as he ran full tilt, barking, and fell in the pit. While I knew we had protective netting there, the audience didn't know that, and there was a gasp. One of the actors scooped him out of the pit, he got applause, and he was fine. A trip to the vet the next day told us that he had severe cataracts in both eyes. When we got him, we knew he had a cataract in one, but the other one was brand new and fully formed. The vet said he was almost blind. I had a choice—I could retire him, or take him to one of the world's best ophthalmologic vets at the Animal Medical Center in New York City. I pulled some strings and got him in. The surgery would cost $5,000, but it was the only hope of restoring Sidney's eyesight.

I figured out that Sidney had learned to follow the smell and sound of the group, fooling us all. When he was outside, he was always on a leash, and in the apartment he memorized his pathways. We had already adopted a corgi named Dory to use as a backup, so we fast-tracked her into Sidney's place. She was young and crazy and upset the pack for a while. Sidney had the surgery and recovered in forty-five days. He could see perfectly and was so happy. To see a dog rediscover the world is like seeing a puppy discover it. We finally got him to the point where he was ready to return to the show, and he came back with a renewed vigor, except for first night—when he went out it was as if he was seeing it for the first time. Then he got very angry he didn't get any treats. The second night, he was still getting pushed away by all the other dogs, and he got really mad. By the third night, his sweet demeanor was gone. He had decided he hated this show and hated show business—he was starting fights with the other dogs backstage. I decided to find him a home with his expensive new eyesight.

I finally put Snickers, one of our cairn terriers who had played Toto, into the pack. After all the scenes in *The Wizard of Oz*, she loved this show—one cue, lots of treats, and then a nap. She thought it was heaven.

Chitty Chitty Bang Bang closed after 285 performances. I had two months left on the apartment lease, and I finally sold the truck at a loss. The dogs had better luck. Our soundman, Scott, came down after every show to visit and play with the dogs. His much-loved pit bull had died, and he became very attached to Harriet. At the end of the run, he asked if he could take her. I was thrilled, except, I explained, Harriet had separation anxiety, and she was bonded to Patches, the beagle. This pit bull from Queens and this beagle from upstate New York ate, played, and slept together. After a short hesitation, Scott and his wife took them both, and those two dogs now have the best lives.

Lady was having a secret love affair with an actor named Dirk. Dirk, his partner, and Lady send Christmas cards to us every year. Fred was adopted by a mystery writer and his wife on the Upper West Side. They really wanted to give a dog a loving home, and when they met Fred, they fell in love with him. Sidney the cocker spaniel went to a young woman who had left her strong-willed cocker at home when she went to college. Sidney reminded her of her old dog, and the two fell in love immediately. Herding Dog Rescue helped us find a home for Dory the corgi. She now lives with a retired couple from Ireland who had corgis all their lives. They live near us in Connecticut, and Dory stops by and visits regularly. Barney, Bard, and Snickers were ours to begin with, and they just came home.

That left one dog, Argyle, the collie. I felt he would never work with me again because of the way he had been frightened, and I felt guilty keeping a dog for myself who wouldn't get the attention that the other working dogs did. I loved that breed so much. I called the rescue group and asked them to find him a home. The day I got the call that they would take Argyle, I went to the kitchen window and looked outside. I saw my seven-year-old daughter playing with him. She was pretending to be a dog trainer, and he was following her all around the yard. She was doing all the commands wrong, but Argyle didn't care. She saw me watching her from the kitchen window and said, "Dad, come here. I trained Argyle." She showed me how he heeled—basically, he followed her. She'd say *Sit*, and push his butt down, and he'd lick her face. She'd throw a ball and say *Fetch*. He'd run, get it, and bring it right back to her, and drop it at her feet. Then she said she wanted to show me his best trick. She told him to pick up the ball, and she led him to a bucket, tapped him on the back of the head, and said *Drop it*—and he did.

For a moment I wondered if this was what I was like with my collie, Rexie. The love that dog was showing Jenna was so sweet that I went in, called the rescue group, thanked them, and said, "He's our collie now."

Chapter 18

Who Are You Calling a Dirty Rat?

In 1996 I was asked to train animals for my first Andrew Lloyd Webber show, a musical based on the British film, *Whistle Down the Wind*, reset in the American South. I had to train two bloodhounds to be handled by actors playing sheriffs as they were chasing criminals. I rescued one bloodhound named Cricket from Bloodhound Rescue of New York, and a bloodhound/coonhound mix named Whitney from a backyard breeder in Connecticut.

The show looked like a sure thing—even bad Andrew Lloyd Webber shows ran for a year. Unfortunately, there were many artistic differences between the creators that could not be resolved, and the show closed out of town. Cricket lived with us until she died of old age. I gave Whitney to my friend Dave. She was a sweet, outgoing dog. In the morning she would get on the local school bus with the kids and was a fixture in Dave's town for years.

In the summer of 2005, I was in Seattle, Washington, setting up the thirtieth-anniversary tour of *Annie*. It was set to run for two years and open in New York in 2007. I find it hard to believe I've been lucky enough to be doing this for thirty years. That August, while we were setting up the show, Dorothy called me from home. Her friend Wendy, who had managed *La Bête*, the show where Dorothy and I met, was representing a London transfer of a new Andrew Lloyd Webber show. It was called *The Woman in White*, a very dark musical based on a book by Wilkie Collins. It was doing well in London, and

Michael Ball, as Count Fosco, with Beatrice in *The Woman in White*. *Photo by Paul Kolnik*

American producers were bringing it here to Broadway. Wendy said there were birds in cages, some mice, and a trained rat. She asked if I would set up the show but allow a production assistant to actually run it.

It was a tough decision, and Dorothy and I discussed it for some time. We were able to get a lot of information about how the animals were used in London—and some of the news was not good. The London trainer had six months to prepare; I would have six weeks. There were stories of birds escaping onstage on opening night and flying around the theater. There were even stories of mice dying because the dry-cleaning chemicals that were used in the costumes were too strong. Based on that information, I thought trying to train a production assistant, probably a college kid, to handle the animals was a bad idea. In the end, concern for the safety of the animals made us decide to go forward, because ignorance is the biggest form of cruelty. With very little enforcement of humane practices on Broadway, there was no telling what might happen if we weren't involved. We agreed to consult in the training of the animals and allow a production assistant to handle them, as long as the person they picked was acceptable to us.

The research we had done showed that the animals in London lived at the theater full-time. The show called for twenty small birds, two larger parrots, four mice that would be trained to stay in your hand, and a rat that would run up and down an actor's arm—on cue. They didn't tell us how they trained them, but we knew all the backstage cues. Dorothy could easily handle the bird setup, and my trainer, Rob Cox, from *Chitty Chitty Bang Bang* had kept pet rats all his adult life. He never trained them, but he thought they made great pets.

The villain who had the rat was played by one of England's foremost musical comedy stars, Michael Ball. He had also been in the London production. The good thing about remounting a show is there is little struggle over the material. All the bugs have been worked out, and you are re-creating the same show with a new cast and a replica of the same set.

My concern was the rat. How could we train the rat so quickly if it took six months in London? I knew rats were very smart, social creatures. They were used for experiments in learning and conditioning, so what could be so hard about training a rat to run up and down someone's arm? I went to the local pet store and bought a book on rats. As I started looking up rat rescue groups, the word came back that Michael Ball wanted to use his London rat. We were asked if we knew anything about flying rats across the Atlantic. It became clear that if someone else's animals were opening the show and we were making less money than usual and getting less than our normal credit, there was no reason for us to do the show at all. I decided to pass.

But when they got the quote from the London trainer on the cost of coming over, they came back to us. By then, time was running short, and I felt training a nonprofessional handler was not practical. They found some extra money to pay one of my handlers. At the time, Rob was lead handler on *Chitty Chitty Bang Bang*. He took a pay cut to work with the rats. He was still living in Brooklyn with the dogs, and I made up the difference in pay for him to continue their care.

"Now for my big finish."
Photo by Paul Kolnik

We got the birds here in Connecticut from a man named Dominic—he works full-time in a factory, but his birds are his passion. When we need a pigeon for *Sesame Street* or a dove for a photo shoot, we usually rent them from him, so he was very happy to help us get twenty canaries. We bought two cockatiels and four mice from a local pet shop. We went on Petfinder .com, and soon we had adopted three rats from Great Pets Rattery and Rescue Center of New York. All three had to go together. Their names were Beatrice and Tabitha, standard white hooded rats, and Charlotte, who was a naked hooded rat. She was all pink and wrinkly, with no hair at all on her body. Talk about weird.

Rats act like hamsters or other small rodents. My daughter, Jenna, loved them, but they made Dorothy uncomfortable—there was something about their scaly, bald tails she didn't like. We brought the rats into New York and met Michael Ball so he could demonstrate some of the cues. He was very upbeat and cordial. He said he wore a fat suit and a full wig in the play, and he demonstrated the move. The rat was supposed to run up his arm to his head, back to his right hand, and then from his right hand to his left hand. I asked about rewards and treats, but Michael said none were ever used. Outside of meeting and making his acquaintance, we really got no information on how to solve the problem, but at least we got the moves for the rats and the mice. The birds always remained in cages.

Rob went on vacation that week, so I started training the rats at home. Using food as a positive reinforcement was the basis of classical conditioning. It works with dogs, so why not on rats? Rob had said they like yogurt treats made especially for rats. Jenna and I began by letting them crawl all over our bodies so they got used to us. Then I began putting the rats on my arms and leading them up my arm, onto my shoulder—where they got a treat—and then down my arm to the other hand, where they got another treat. In three days, they were going completely each way.

Rob had warned us that they have very sharp little teeth and might nibble to explore their environment. Rule number one in owning a rat is do not stick your fin-

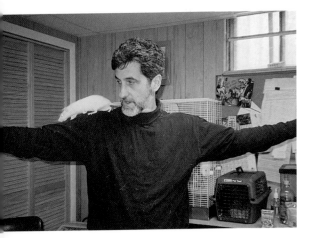

Michael Ball looked much more comfortable doing this.

ger inside the cage. A rat will see it and nibble it to investigate. Rule number two is when you're handling them, make sure you wash your hands so that you have no food matter on them, or they will nibble your fingers.

The director of the show, Trevor Nunn, is known around the world, and I was looking forward to meeting him. I finally got the chance in late September after a rehearsal. I showed him the white rats and Charlotte, the naked rat, who happened to be the best trained. He laughed and said while they certainly wanted a little repulsion factor with the image of the rat crawling over Michael, the naked rat was taking it a bit too far. When we showed him the behaviors, he said, "We cannot use food at all because they would bite the actors." I assured him that with proper hygiene and handling, it wouldn't be a problem, but he was adamant. The trainers in London were insistent because they feared for the actor's safety. It was a challenge. I guaranteed him the rats would not bite the actors. He smiled a slight smile and said, "Would you bet your job on it?" Without waiting a beat, I said, "Yes."

He said he would be very impressed if I succeeded, and said if it were true, it would have saved them a lot of money in London. It would be the last time that we would have a chance to speak for the rest of the run, but I had bet my reputation on a rat. Now, practically speaking, I kept trying to figure out the problem. When you pick up the treat, you get the scent on your hands. If you don't feed the rats fast enough, the rats will bite your fingers trying to get the treat. I kept trying to figure out ways to handle the food and the rat at the same time—then it came to me. Could a rat learn to do a series of behaviors that began in its cage and ended in its cage? They learned very fast, and within a week I had taught them to go from their cage to my right hand, to my left, then back to their cage, where they were rewarded with a treat.

To prepare Michael, we would give him some hand sanitizer before he went on. He could then handle the rat, drop the treat in the top of the onstage cage, never having to touch the rat with food on his hands. It worked like a charm. The rat never nibbled us at all. The mice were actually harder because they were not as smart, and they got stressed. We used magic markers on their tails to tell them apart. The calmest mouse had one stripe, two stripes for the next calmest, and so on. We would place them on our palms, and when they moved to the edge of our hands, we would touch their heads with our thumbs. They learned very quickly that if they wanted to avoid being touched, they just had to sit in the palms of our hands.

Dorothy secured all the birds in the proper cages and we were ready to go. A special dressing room was outfitted at the theater, the Marriott Marquis on Times Square. We were given the only dressing room in the entire theater with windows, so the animals could have natural light, and a special thermostat was installed so we could keep it climate controlled. We filed all the health permits with the City of New York, a vet came to inspect the premises, and we were finally all set.

We began rehearsals in late September 2005, which gave us two weeks to work with the actors and the rats in the studio. We set up the animals in the theater to get used to their surroundings, and then every day we would walk through Times Square with rats in cat cages, always drawing stares. We began the technical rehearsals in mid-October, with previews starting at the end of the month. The crew at the Marquis was great at building a booth offstage where we could bring the birds and transfer them to the show cages. It was completely sealed off so that if one of them escaped, they could be contained in the room. The first previews went great for the animals.

Between Michael Ball being so comfortable onstage in the role and the rats being so good, it worked very well. Beatrice the white rat was the star. Charlotte, the naked rat, though best at the behavior, was relegated to being the understudy by the director. The birds and the rat appeared at the end of the second act, when Michael Ball's villainous character is packing to leave town. At that point he sings a comedic song to his furry and feathered friends. The last note of his song is sung to the rat. Beatrice was housed onstage in a glass terrarium with a hinged lid. At the appointed time, Michael would go over, lift the lid, take Beatrice out, extend his arms, do the behavior, drop her back into the terrarium, drop her treat in and close the lid.

At the fourth public performance, Michael accidentally closed the lid on the end of Beatrice's tail. This was the first time in thirty years that one of my animals had been hurt onstage, and it was deeply upsetting. When we got Beatrice offstage, there was a lot of blood and she was obviously in pain and distress. We rushed her to the emergency veterinary clinic. Fortunately, nature gave rats tails that break off easily if a predator gets them. She had lost the very tip of her tail, and needed only a few stitches.

Charlotte took over in true "the rat must go on" tradition, and did great the next day. It took a week for Beatrice's tail to heal and for her to regain her confidence, but she made it for opening night. That was nothing compared to our leading lady, Maria Friedman. During the technical rehearsals she felt a lump on her breast—it was breast cancer. The show had been produced for her in London by her sister, Sonia, the score had been written for her voice, and the show had been directed around her. She was brilliant in the role. She had surgery while her understudy learned and covered the role. Maria battled back and also made it back for opening night. This is the stuff of Broadway legends.

The show was not well received by the New York critics. I got a lot of good publicity as "The Rat Man," while having two shows running on Broadway at the same time. They overlapped by six weeks before *Chitty Chitty Bang Bang* closed. CBS *Evening News* even did a piece on me. They came and photographed the rats, the dogs in *Chitty*, my work with the Humane Society, and my family life at home.

Our agreement with the producers was that we got a reduced fee until the show had been running for a year. *The Woman in White* closed after three months and 109 performances. At the end of the run, the canaries went back to Dominic. We gave the cockatiels to a friend who was homebound. The mice, having a fairly short life span, lived with us for the rest of their days. Rob kept the rats. Our star rat, Beatrice, lasted the longest. Being a star on Broadway gave her something to live for.

Chapter 19

A Case of Mistaken Identity

September 2005 was a busy month. At the Hilton Theater we had eight dogs working in *Chitty Chitty Bang Bang*. We had a room full of rats, mice, and birds at *The Woman in White*. Our plate was full with some really difficult tasks. Little did I know a bloodbath was waiting just around the corner.

In October I got a call from Melinda Burke, who was the general manager of an off-Broadway theater called the Atlantic Theater Company. They were looking to do the American premiere of a new play, *The Lieutenant of Inishmore*, by the Irish playwright Martin McDonagh. It was currently playing in London. Three of McDonagh's previous plays, *The Beauty Queen of Leenane, The Lonesome West,* and *The Pillowman*, had all played on Broadway and received Tony Award nominations for best play. The theater company wanted to get this play up and move it to Broadway almost immediately.

"What kind of animal do you need?" I asked. Melinda said, "A black cat." A shiver ran up my spine. I was currently dealing with rats, and I hadn't trained a cat for a show in more than twenty years. I asked what the play was about. She said it was about an Irish terrorist who finds out his cat is dead and murders all the people involved.

"Is it a drama?" I asked. "Oh no," she said. "It's a comedy." A comedy, she continued, where four people get killed and chopped up onstage. At that point I was thinking this was some sort of practical joke or something.

Peter Gerety, as Donny, and Domhnall Gleeson, as Davey, with a prop cat in *The Lieutenant of Inishmore*. *Photo by Monique Carboni*

She went on to say that the cat comes out in the last two minutes of the play and just eats some food. "But you should know we do kill two cats onstage during the play." Before I could even get the words out of my mouth, she said, "But they're fake, and it's done in good taste."

Now I was seeing red. How could any violence to an animal be funny or in good taste? My whole tone changed. I told her I was a representative of the Humane Society of New York and could not be part of something that depicts violence to animals. Again Melinda apologized and asked that before I turned it down, would I please read the play. She said I would probably change my mind. I had no desire to read it, except to find out what they were doing and form some sort of protest. I agreed, and she overnighted the script. The next day when it arrived, I read it and I was intrigued. The violence was over the top—based in reality, but exaggerated by the playwright to show the worst in man's nature—and the dead cats were obviously puppets. The dialogue was hysterical.

A mad IRA terrorist leaves his beloved cat with his dad. When a neighbor brings a dead cat from the road to the dad, they both worry that the terrorist will come back and find out. Ultimately the terrorist does return and is going to kill them both when three members of a rival gang come along and capture him. His girlfriend helps him escape and kill his rivals. In the final scene, the dad and the neighbor are chopping up the bodies while the terrorist mourns the loss of his cat. The girlfriend finds out the terrorist mistakenly killed her cat. She kills him and leaves. As the dad and neighbor remain, they look up and at that moment the terrorist's cat walks in through a hole in the wall and starts to eat. All the violence was for nothing. The two remaining men put a gun to the cat's head to kill him, but realize there's been enough bloodshed for one day as the final curtain comes down. When I read the final twist I was hooked. If we could reassure the audience no cats were harmed, it could be a smash hit.

I had heard wonderful things about the Atlantic Theater. Their track record of fostering new theater was admirable, but mostly they were good guys. Off-Broadway pays less than half of what Broadway pays, and you either have to be rich or very poor to work there. After I read the play, I wanted to be part of this theatrical event.

I actually had a great black cat. His name was Mr. Ed. I was doing a production of *Annie* in upstate New York in the summer of 1995. The theater had put me up in an inn attached to a dairy farm. One morning, as I was walking the Sandy dogs, this big black cat came strolling right up to us. He rubbed on my legs, purred, rubbed on the dogs, and just said hello. Neither the dogs nor I could believe this bold cat would just stroll up to us. Each morning he would come out to say hello and follow us for our walk. I enjoyed his company, so the day before I left, I asked the innkeeper's wife if the cat belonged to anyone. She told me that the dairy attracted cats from all over the county. They were a nuisance, and they tried to get rid of them. I didn't want to think about the methods they might use. I called Dorothy and told her about this cat. I said, "He's not afraid of dogs, he's friendly with people, and he's really not afraid of anything. Maybe we could use him in show business." She said it was up to me, but she didn't want another cat in the house. We already had two. He could be a barn cat.

The next day I threw the cat in the back of the van and drove home. Knowing he would be living in the barn, I tried to think of a funny name for him. I came up with Mr. Ed. That way, when people heard us calling him, instead of a horse coming out of the barn, they'd see this cat. When I got home, I showed him to Dorothy. She was pretty impressed with him, and when I told her his name she made me promise not to name any more animals.

The first night we made a nice bed for him in our tack room with pillow, litter box, and food. The barn was about 200 feet from our house. All night long he howled and cried. It kept us awake, but I thought he'd adjust. The next day we let him out, and he spent the day investigating the yard. He came to the back door and tried to come in. We kept pushing him back, pushing him back. The second night, the same thing, meowing all night long. The third night, I thought maybe he didn't like being locked up all night, so I left the tack-room door open. Within fifteen minutes he was outside our back door, meowing bloody murder. At about 3:00 A.M., I got up and said, "All right, you win. Come sleep in the kitchen."

In another fifteen minutes, he was at our bedroom door. Dorothy said, "No way—he's a barn cat, not an indoor cat." But, at that point, even the dogs sleeping in the bedroom had had enough. I opened the door; Mr. Ed jumped up on the bed, kneaded a spot between us, and went to sleep. He was never asked to sleep outside again, except when he tried to sneak out and do some hunting.

As it turned out, Mr. Ed was so outgoing, he ultimately did have a great photo career. He posed for jigsaw puzzles and advertisements. He was a photo standby for Salem, the cat from the television series *Sabrina, The Teenage Witch*. But his crowning achievement was in the year 2000, when he appeared on the cover of *Sports Illustrated*. People have said for years that there's a curse to being featured on the cover, and they wanted to jinx the curse. That cover was shown on *Today* and other network shows. Mr. Ed was clearly a star, but to us he was just one great cat. Not only could he handle the dogs and the other cats, but he loved people.

When Jenna was born, he gravitated to her. As she became a toddler, he would be in her room. She loved him because he was the only stuffed animal that moved. As a preschooler, she dressed him up in doll clothes. He sat there with a humiliated scowl, but he would never leave. Besides being a great model, he was also a great pet.

He loved food. So this show would be a snap for him. In mid-October I set up a meeting with the producers, the director, the playwright, and Mr. Ed. I was told that in the London production, the cat kept escaping and running outside. The cat in the London production was shy, but came out just long enough to eat. They showed me a mock-up of the set in the rehearsal room. Mr. Ed would enter through a chute that led through a small opening, which closed behind him, to a shelf about five feet off the stage. Then he would have to eat and stay calm during the scene, including when the actors held a gun to his head and then petted him. One of the actors would grab him and exit during the final blackout. I told them all about Mr. Ed and said that given the short amount of rehearsal time, a pro like him would make it happen. We even tried the shelf, and Mr. Ed walked around it, surveying the room. A great sense of relief came over them because he wasn't frightened.

When an $8 million Broadway show says that they don't have a budget for the animals, it's a joke. But this was off-Broadway, and there was very little money. They have apprentices working backstage and people who donate their time to make shows happen. I explained that they would need to hire one of my handlers and pay at least what the actors were making. Kirsten, one of my trainers from *Chitty Chitty Bang Bang*, agreed to do the job at the reduced rate, and then go to Broadway with it. She was interested to see how we would train a cat. I would take a reduced weekly fee. It was understood that if the show moved to Broadway, I would go with it and our rates would increase. Mr. Ed would live at the theater, and Kirsten would go in every day to care for him, saving transportation costs. Rehearsals were going to begin in January 2006, with the first performance in February. I wanted to be in a week before opening to get Mr. Ed used to the backstage area—and to the idea that the stage was his new home and the shelf his dinner spot. It was an exciting project after the commercial failure of *Chitty Chitty Bang Bang*.

I had six weeks to get Mr. Ed ready. I had built a mock shelf in my downstairs office to begin feeding Mr. Ed. During that time we prepped and opened *The Woman in White*, and we also closed and had to dismantle *Chitty Chitty Bang Bang*. Then I could focus on *Inishmore*.

The Atlantic Theater is in an old church. The upstairs was turned into the wardrobe and actors' area, and the stage level had two workrooms behind the stage. One was an office, and the other was walled in half, so Ed could have one side and the maintenance of the dismembered bodies took the other side. Our side had a large window that overlooked a courtyard, so Ed could watch birds and squirrels.

When we began our two session days, we would bring Ed onstage at lunchtime, when the work had stopped, and put him on the shelf. He needed to see nothing in the space would harm him, and we fed him there. Then we did the same at night when it was quiet. Basically, Ed thought it was the largest kitchen he had ever seen. During the performance, Ed would mostly be handled by a great actor named Peter Gerety. Peter and I had worked together fifteen years earlier for the New York Shakespeare Festival in Central Park. Peter appeared in *Two Gentlemen of Verona*, the only Shakespeare play that has a role written in it for a dog. Peter worked with my first Toto, Bugsy. They did a comedic scene that brought the house down every show. When I saw him at rehearsals for *Inishmore*, we hugged, and he told me that he still had Bugsy's picture on his refrigerator. Peter loved cats, and he fell in love with Ed. Who wouldn't? He was the perfect cat, and he could act. After three days of Peter coming to our dressing room and playing, which was the highlight of his day, we put Ed on. Between Ed's demeanor and Peter's love for animals, it worked flawlessly. It was a huge weight lifted off the shoulders of our producers, director, and writer. Ed's entrance was the pivotal moment in resolving this mass murder play about mistaken cat identity. Things were great even up to dress rehearsal.

Our first preview came and the theater was packed. I watched from the front as the play took us on an emotional roller-coaster ride. When Ed entered, the audience screamed, gasped, and laughed—it was unlike any reaction I had ever seen in the theater. The laughter went on for over a minute. It was truly a cathartic moment, when all the tension that had been built up was released. I saw Ed react, which I had expected him to do, but then I watched with worry as he became more and more concerned. He had a fearful look on his face. I realized the release of the audience's tension must have sent a shock wave onstage.

The lights went out, Peter grabbed Ed, and the play ended. When the director said all the cat had to do was walk out on a shelf and eat some food, he neglected to say that the audience becomes unglued. At the production meeting after the show, I said I wished I had been warned of this reaction, so we could have prepared Ed with a laugh track, to desensitize him to the sound. I had our sound designer do exactly that the next day, and we began using it. But the damage was already done. The next night Ed went out, then turned around to come back through the hole. The third night, he sat there and cried. We played the laugh track for hours in his room, and onstage, and by the weekend, he got over it. Now the theater had become the biggest and loudest kitchen he had ever eaten in.

The reviews were positive, and the run was hugely successful—a sellout for all nine weeks. Except for the first week, Ed was flawless and everyone was amazed, but I got no credit. Obviously, if my name was out in front of the theater or in the program, people would know there was a live animal in the show and that would spoil the surprise. Unlike shows whose producers said I wasn't important enough to get credit, this show told me I was *too* well known to get credit. I gladly agreed to a plaque being placed in the lobby at the end of the show, with Mr. Ed's photo and my credits.

After opening, they moved forward, planning the move to Broadway. The set was transferred intact. Ed had the exact same place to perform each night. In the meantime, a Broadway show would require an understudy. At the Humane Society of New York, we had received a group of cats and dogs displaced by Hurricane Katrina. Among them was a black cat named Fairfax. While he was in our hospital recuperating, he talked constantly, and would reach out of his cage to play with everyone.

"I'm the live one."

He had survived a hurricane, confinement, transport to New York City, and was still willing to play—I felt doing a show would be nothing for him.

But putting these two tomcats together would be like putting two divas together—one huge catfight. The day after we closed at the Atlantic Theater, Kirsten and I moved Ed and Fairfax to the Lyceum Theater, where they had separate dressing rooms. We had to have the crew build playscapes for the cats because the rooms were so small, and they had to install full spectrum lights on timers because there were no windows.

While Ed settled into his dressing room, Fairfax screamed for attention so much that they could hear him onstage. At first the crew put sound-proofing foam all over the inside of his dressing room. The next day we came in to find it shredded to bits. It looked like there had been a black snowstorm. Fairfax seemed grateful we had given him a new toy to shred. Finally, we decided that in the first act, we'd put a harness on Fairfax and sit with him in the basement with all the actors and crew, to wear him out. They played with him to the point of exhaustion. The wardrobe room had a shelf that looked like the one in the play, so Kirsten asked the wardrobe supervisor, Nancy, if we could practice on it. During each show, Fairfax would walk into Nancy's room, do his little bit, get fed, and move on.

We began getting Ed used to the new theater. While his shelf was exactly the same, the room, its airflow, and feel were much different. From day one we had the sound department play his laugh track at a very loud level to mimic the bigger audience. And with Peter Gerety holding a gun to his head every night, then loving him up, he got right back into the routine. We began previews in late April and opened in May. The reviews were again great but warned people about the extreme gore. Only one review spoke of the cat.

We were very popular with the younger crowd, and they tried to make a go at a long run, but the sad fact is on Broadway, a play that gets good reviews and wins prizes usually closes for lack of audience. In the last two weeks before closing, the two original actors from London (who had done the Atlantic Theater production and the Broadway opening) had their visas expire, and they had to leave. The young man who was in the scene with Peter and Ed was replaced by his understudy. His rhythm and energy were totally different from the first actor's, and it was just different enough that after eight months of voluntarily going onstage, Ed decided he didn't like this actor's performance and wouldn't go out. In the best tradition of "the cat must go on," Fairfax stepped in. We all were nervous. Imagine a cat having no experience, going on cold. But outside of being too happy and animated, Fairfax went on and closed the run.

Nancy, in the wardrobe department, was so taken by Fairfax—and the fact that we couldn't have another male cat at home—that it led to the perfect adoption for this Katrina refugee. Fairfax is living happily in New Jersey with Nancy's other cat and two dogs.

But now I have to let you in on a theatrical secret, one not even known by the show's producers or creative team. In a case of life imitating art, we had a case of mistaken cat identity, because the cat that performed in the show was not the cat that auditioned for it. If you reread this chapter, you'll see I talk about introducing "Mr. Ed" to the producers and writer, but then I call the cat "Ed" during rehearsals and performances. Two days after the audition, Mr. Ed started vomiting and losing weight. After another two days, we took him over to our vet. He was diagnosed with that catchall phrase, *irritable bowel syndrome*. My vet prescribed a little cortisone to calm his bowels, but it didn't work. More tests showed scarring on his intestines. A simple surgery could remove the scarring, and after that, he should be fine.

While I was assured Mr. Ed would recover, I decided we needed to look for a backup. We tried for a month to nurse Mr. Ed back to health. Although his spirits were good, he'd become skin and bones. Dorothy and I went online to Petfinder.com and found a cat in a municipal shelter in Connecticut. It was two weeks before our first rehearsal. I drove down to see the cat. I wasn't thrilled with the cat I had seen online, but I saw another black cat in a cage nearby. He was a big male. The card said he had been found as a stray with a leg injury. With the infection from his leg injury cured, he was ready for adoption. They had named him George.

I took him out and he stretched, purred, hung out with the other cats meowing and dogs barking. I decided to take him out of desperation. We set him up in my basement office because he didn't get along with other cats. I began feeding him on our shelf, and in fourteen days, I brought him to New York City. We had decided telling this group we were bringing in an inexperienced cat would cause undue worry—but, as far as I was concerned, this stray had as much chance of succeeding as the real Mr. Ed, because, as I always say, there is no such thing as a trained cat.

At home Dorothy and I started calling the new cat "George Eddie" so he would come when you called him Ed. George Eddie did the entire off-Broadway run and ultimately made it to Broadway, as described. After the show, George Eddie came back to my office to live. We tried incorporating him with our three other cats, but it didn't work. It wasn't fair to such a great cat to keep him in my office, so we placed him with a wonderful public relations agent we had worked with in New York City. She had moved to New York, bought a condo, and missed her dogs but couldn't have one with her lifestyle. One day she said to me, "If they only made cats that act like dogs." I said, "Boy, do I have a cat for you!" George Eddie now lives in that condo in New York City. Mr. Ed held on until July 2006—he was a great cat, and we miss him dearly.

So that's the true story. To the producers, directors, and playwright of *The Lieutenant of Inishmore*—well, this time the joke's on you. We provided a cat that was not the cat you hired to play the role of a cat whose mistaken identity causes mayhem.

Chapter 20

Get with The Group

With *Chitty Chitty Bang Bang* closing, *The Woman in White* running, and our involvement in *The Lieutenant of Inishmore*, I couldn't have felt more proud of our animals and the work we did. Unfortunately, though, all of the shows listed above were transfers from the English stage. Theater is theater, but I longed for a good, old-fashioned American musical. What presented itself was a good, old-fashioned American drama.

In mid-December 2005, Melanie Weintraub called from the management office of Lincoln Center. They were doing a production of *Awake and Sing!*, generally considered the finest work by American playwright Clifford Odets. Lincoln Center was honoring both the work of Odets and the famous Group Theatre. Harold Clurman, Cheryl Crawford, and Lee Strasberg founded The Group Theatre in 1931. Their ambition was to transform American theater by creating an acting ensemble that would present powerful, naturalistic works. Although it lasted only ten years, The Group Theatre was very influential, particularly among actors. That's because The Group wanted to break down the line between life and acting onstage. Actors were to actually *feel* the emotions their characters were having every moment of the play. In order to do this, they created their own acting style,

Ben Gazzara, as Jacob Berger, with Barney in Lincoln Center Theater's production of *Awake and Sing!*
Photo by Paul Kolnik

called The Method, which was an Americanized version of the Stanislav-sky Method developed at the Moscow Arts Theatre. Other famous original members of The Group Theatre included Stella Adler and Sanford Meisner. Students of The Group Theatre included Marlon Brando, Paul Newman, Al Pacino, Meryl Streep, and many others.

I've always felt the reason animals are so appealing onstage is that they are the ultimate Method actors. Animals onstage are always in the moment. While human actors have to strive to be real onstage, animals *are* real—and that's what I believe makes it so exciting for an audience to watch an animal onstage.

To re-create the feel of the original production, this revival was going to be presented at the Belasco Theater, where *Awake and Sing!* was originally produced fifty-one years earlier, rather than at Lincoln Center. It would open almost in the same month. The set was being replicated with modern updates. Famed director Bartlett Sher, who had just directed *The Light in the Piazza* for Lincoln Center, would be directing *Awake and Sing!* The cast featured many talented performers, including Zoe Wanamaker, Ben Gazzara, and Mark Ruffalo.

Awake and Sing! was written during the height of the Great Depression. It was a comedy/drama about a Jewish family trying to stay afloat in the 1930s, and raised the question: What is life for? What I found unusual was not the fact that the family in the play had a dog, but rather, the breed they chose. The script called for a miniature white poodle to play Tootsie, the grandfather's dog. In all the research they had done for the show, there was absolutely nothing on the origin of the dog—who owned it, who handled it, why they chose a poodle, since a poor family wouldn't be able to afford a purebred dog during the Depression.

Being familiar with The Method from my studies with Stella Adler, I could imagine that a Group member had had a dog at the time, and Harold Clurman put it onstage as an exercise to keep the actors in the moment. If you don't know what a dog will do in a scene, then you have to focus. When Melanie said the script called for a messy white poodle, I said, "I don't have a white one, but I have a black one with a résumé." I was referring to our old friend Barney. Since Lincoln Center is a nonprofit, I thought the cost savings of using a dog I already owned would be attractive. An audition was set up for Barney at Lincoln Center. It was actually a people audition, and actors were coming and going. In fact, I saw a cast member from *Chitty Chitty Bang Bang* there. He asked what I was doing—I told him Barney had an audition. Ultimately Barney got the job and the other cast member didn't.

We went into the audition room and met Bartlett and the casting director for Lincoln Center. Barney was very outgoing and friendly in that poodle-ish sort of way. Then I demonstrated how he could do all the basic commands. They liked him, but they weren't crazy about his color. They really wanted to stick with the script as it was written. When I explained the cost and trouble of acquiring a new poodle, they decided Barney would be fine.

Bartlett then explained the first cue was Barney entering and jumping up on Ben Gazzara. His next cue was to come out to Mark Ruffalo, and for his final cue, he exits up a staircase with Ben. It sounded pretty simple. I explained the need to bond with the actors, especially since the set had walls and I couldn't command him from the wings. Bart said he needed the dog well trained so the actors could concentrate. That didn't make sense to me. I tried explaining how my training techniques sought to create a real bond with the actors so the audience would see the reality, but apparently the new Method didn't include dogs.

Because Barney was only in those three short scenes, they didn't need us to come in at the beginning. The acting company would need a chance to bond and get to know one another. Rehearsals began in mid-February in the studios at Lincoln Center—we started in early March, two weeks before the first public performance. Rob, my trainer from *The Woman in White*, agreed to handle Barney. *The Woman in White* had closed and the salary for *Awake and Sing!* was better than unemployment. Rob would bring Barney in each day on the subway in a dog-carry bag to save the theater money.

The first day for me was very exciting—I had always dreamed of working with a cast of this stature. Also, the production stage manager, Bob Bennett, was an old friend. Bob was the original production stage manager of the Goodspeed production of *Annie* the summer I found the original Sandy. We hadn't worked together in thirty years, but Bob had followed my career with pride. He understood what I needed and tried to accommodate it. That day, we also met Ben Gazzara, an amazing actor who owns dachshunds. He was working very hard on his character in the play. He actually knew some of the original members of The Group Theatre, and we spoke about the old days, with everyone listening. The other actor who handled Barney was Mark Ruffalo. He was making his Broadway debut, having had a great film career. He loved dogs, was a down-to-earth type of guy, and got down on the floor and just loved Barney up.

At our first rehearsal, we were blocking the show. Bartlett seemed a little distant. I got the feeling he didn't enjoy wasting time blocking the dog. I tried to be as professional as possible—having studied The Method myself, I wanted to know the motivation for the scene so I could devise a behavior that seemed natural. Barney would enter from a room upstage, about halfway into the first act. I asked if there was a way to wait in that room with Barney. They said no, because the set had four walls. I explained that a dog couldn't wait in a dark room for twenty minutes and enter on cue, so either Rob would have to be there with him, or a trapdoor would have to be installed. We all decided the trapdoor was the better option.

When you rehearse in a big rehearsal room, walls and scenery are indicated by tape on the floor so the actors can approximate their moves. Barney had to enter from that room and go downstage to Ben, who was sitting in a chair. At first, without the wall, Barney just walked across the tape. The director said he couldn't step over the tape. It seemed kind of silly to me to have to explain that the dog didn't know there was a wall there, so we just got some cardboard boxes and made fake walls. Barney was supposed to run to Ben, uncued. I explained he would need a cue or a treat from Ben onstage. At first Bart was resistant, but when Ben spoke up and said he thought his character would have goodies in his pocket to spoil the dog, the problem was solved.

The other two scenes were easy to stage but, again, I didn't feel very welcomed by the company. Rob and I would come in on their lunch breaks to work the pattern in the room with Barney, and then we would steal moments with the cast members when they weren't onstage. They had become a very close-knit group, which is part of The Method, but by excluding me and Barney, they were missing the point about him needing to be familiar with everyone.

About the fourth day in of the cold-shoulder treatment, I needed to do something, so I asked Bob if I could make an announcement. He said I could have three minutes. I introduced myself to the group and said what an honor it was to be there. I could see eyes roll. Then I said, "It's especially moving for me, having studied acting with Stella Adler." Everyone perked up. I explained she would have understood the cast having a relationship on- and offstage with the dog, to help with the reality. I invited everyone to say hello to us at any time, and we would help facilitate it. I thanked everyone and went back to our spot.

The cast had a new respect for me. Not only was I familiar with The Method, I had studied with one of the original cast members. It was during that brief time after *Annie* had closed at Goodspeed but before it opened on Broadway. I moved to Greenwich Village with Sandy and entered New York University. I had chosen Stella Adler's conservatory as part of my university training. She instilled a great respect for the theater but also told us to respect ourselves, which I never forgot. Mark Ruffalo came up to me and said he had studied with her, too, and we started trading stories. Even Bartlett every now and then would come and ask me for my opinion of a scene.

We moved to the Belasco Theater one week later. We had a beautiful old-time box set that also had the ability to fly out the walls as the play progressed. The union crew guys at the Belasco were very accommodating. They had set up a dressing room for us in the basement. There was a lot of history in that theater. They talked about the ghosts there, and showed us an old pulley system that Houdini had installed to make an elephant disappear.

It took Barney a couple of days to learn his path through the set to Ben. It's one thing to be in an open rehearsal room, hiding behind some cardboard boxes, but quite another to enter through a trapdoor onto a room onstage, wait for another door to open, and then run to someone. By the first preview Barney had it. His second cue with Mark was flawless, and for his third cue, Ben carried him up a flight of stairs. Unfortunately, the theater was so small they couldn't get escape stairs there for Ben, so Rob had to climb up a ladder to retrieve Barney so he wouldn't have to spend the whole third act up in the air. There was no curtain call for Barney, so we got to leave early.

The second day of rehearsal, we heard barking coming from Ben's dressing room. Bob the stage manager investigated and found that Ben had brought his dachshund along to keep him company. This presented two problems. First, we had tried to make Barney think he was special in Ben's eyes—but having Ben's dog in his dressing room meant we couldn't visit. The second problem was that you could hear Ben's dog barking onstage. It distracted Barney and the other actors as well. It was only the second day, and it was an honest mistake. The next day, Rob took Barney to visit Ben. He knocked on his door and Ben said to come in. As Barney rushed in, Ben's dog ran up and bit Barney. Quick reflexes on Rob's part prevented anyone from getting hurt. It seems Ben really loved his dog and was hoping we could get the dachshund and Barney to be friends. Ben felt very bad about the accident and didn't bring his dog to the theater after that.

Each night before the show, Barney would make his rounds. All the dressing rooms were up five flights of stairs. Thirty minutes before the show started, Rob would lead Barney from dressing room to dressing room for a quick hello. Ben and Mark gave him special treats, and Barney would run to their doors, bark, and scratch. The script called for an unkempt poodle, so we let Barney's hair grow out. By the time we closed, he looked like a mop.

The show opened in mid-April, got great reviews, and won the Tony Award for Best Revival of a Play. There was talk of extending the run, but just like *The Lieutenant of Inishmore*, serious drama can't make money on Broadway. As planned, they had a limited run of ninety-two performances and closed in June. For a few weeks I could watch the first and second acts of *Awake and Sing!* to see Barney perform, then walk over to *Inishmore* for the last bit with Ed the cat.

The year between 2005 and 2006 helped enhance my reputation as the "go-to" trainer for Broadway shows, but I couldn't help wondering—where was the next *Annie*? Where was the show about a girl and her dog that would run a long time?

Chapter 21

Phi Beta Bruiser

In the summer of 2005, I was in St. Louis for a production of *Annie*. I was invited to lunch with Mike Isaacson, a producer from Fox Theatricals who had worked with my wife, Dorothy, and become friendly. Now, animal trainers aren't often asked to "do lunch," but people in the theater never turn down a free meal. He told me that his group was partnering with two New York producers to do a musical based on the movie *Legally Blonde*, which featured a Chihuahua in a key role. There was also a small part for an English bulldog. Mike was representing the other producers and asked if I would be interested in working on the show.

For that brief moment in St. Louis, I felt after thirty years, I had arrived—I was being asked to be part of the team in the early stages of a new show. I said I was honored, and asked if there were any plans. He explained they were going to take the old-fashioned route of a reading first, then a workshop in New York. If it came together, there would be an out-of-town tryout and, finally, Broadway. It's much more expensive, but it's much less risky than trying to open immediately on Broadway. I was all for this.

In November I received an invitation to the reading of *Legally Blonde* in New York. In the movie, Bruiser, the Chihuahua, is the constant companion of Elle Woods, the lead character. As the musical opens, the sorority girls

Annaleigh Ashford, as Margot, with Chico in *Legally Blonde*. *Photo by Paul Kolnik, courtesy of the*
Broadway production of Legally Blonde The Musical

can't find Elle. Bruiser comes running to center stage, tapping a character on the leg and having a five-line "conversation" with her, where he barks, and she listens. He was indicated in scenes when she gets to Harvard. He growled at Elle's romantic rival. In the second act, Bruiser helps Elle win her case by barking when a witness is lying, and then pulling a shower curtain back and forth to reveal a plot point.

My initial reaction was that it was an upbeat, fun, high-energy musical. My second thought was all the barking wouldn't work. Remember, on film you only have to get it right once—onstage, it's a totally different story. Never in theater history had a dog had "lines." Sandy barked on cue in *Annie* and *Annie Warbucks*, but we accomplished that by directing the whole scene around the dog, and it was only one line, not five.

In January 2006 I was contacted by the producers to officially work on the show. I was told there would be a workshop in May. Workshops in New York could be very costly, but they give the creative team and potential investors a chance to see the show on its feet. For this workshop, the producers felt there would be no time to focus on the dogs. I explained how much money and time they could save if I was involved. I promised I wouldn't take any rehearsal time away, but acclimating the dogs, plus giving the director a chance to see how a dog looks in a scene, would be very helpful. They agreed, and in February we began our search for Bruiser.

In March I had my first face-to-face meeting with Jerry Mitchell, the director. Jerry and I are about the same age and came to New York at about the same time. He was a dancer who had worked his way up from the chorus. He had specific ideas for Bruiser, but he had never really worked with animals onstage. I felt we needed two dogs, like I had used in several other shows—an active dog to do the barking behaviors, and then a very calm, quiet dog that could easily be held or carried onstage for long periods of time without stealing focus away from the actors. We agreed that this would be a good place to start, and then he could plug them in during the workshop as a test. As for the bulldog, she would run onstage and get picked up by one of the actresses and carried off.

I had never trained dogs this small for the stage that weren't carried around. Little dogs don't realize they have been shrunk by man's breeding. They have the same DNA as a wolf, so they perceive the world as a place filled with giants. They can be either frightened messes or dogs with Napoleonic complexes. The quiet dog was easy. The active dog would need to think he was a Great Dane. I needed a dog with enough self-confidence to come out onstage and bark repeatedly in front of two thousand people, an orchestra, and a company of actors. But dogs that have that kind of courage usually are aggressive as well.

We turned to Petfinder.com, and the two most promising Chihuahuas were in New Jersey. Petfinder.com said the Associated Humane Society had a young, outgoing male named Chico. Not far from Newark, a rescue group had an eight-month-old named Taco. I made arrangements to drive the four hours to New Jersey to see both dogs.

I met Chico first. He had been surrendered by an elderly couple who said their grandchildren were allergic to him. As a result, Chico had been tied out in their yard in Newark and thought he was a guard dog. When I arrived I was met by Roseann Trezza, an old friend who was now president of the shelter. When she heard I was coming, she checked the dog and was not pleased. He was was young and healthy, but so "outgoing" that he bit the staff. It was not the information I wanted to hear, but I decided to look at the dog anyway.

The staff warned me that Chico didn't like treats, didn't like to be touched, and would lunge at me. As I came into his sight, he was sitting at the back of his cage. Alert, defiant, he immediately started barking. The workers said he needed to be lassoed to get him out of the cage, but he liked to go for long walks. The guys gave me a leash and stepped back. I walked up to the cage and he went back, growling. I leaned onto the cage with my back to him and held the door open with my left hand. After a minute or so he stopped barking. I started talking to him soothingly. I wasn't yelling, I wasn't reaching in, and I wasn't grabbing. In another minute he tiptoed over to me. I didn't move because he was right near my face. He

Photo by Paul Kolnik, courtesy of the Broadway production of Legally Blonde The Musical

sniffed, I looked at him and he retreated, barking. I kept up my talking and put my hand out, and he came over to sniff it, and then jumped into the crook of my arm.

After a few more minutes I was able to pet him. I slipped the leash over his head. I took a glance around and there was a crowd of people watching in disbelief. As I tightened the leash around his neck, he freaked. I quickly put him on the ground, at which time he lunged at the staff. I let him lead me to the door. Chico dragged me down the street, barking at everyone to get out of his way, trying to bite the tires of tractor-trailers, marking to let the world know that he was there. After about five minutes, I knelt down and he did something totally unexpected. He came to my side, sat down, and leaned into me. He wanted to touch me, but when I brought my hand down to pet him, he growled. He wanted contact with humans but didn't know how to accept it. In that moment my heart said to me, *This dog deserves a second chance*, even if my head said *Never use a biting dog in a show*.

In my mind I knew he would probably be put down. The small biters are a liability to the reputation and security of animal shelters. Roseann apologized for wasting my time. I interrupted her and said, "I'd like to give him a try."

She looked at me in disbelief. "You always say you can't take biting dogs."

"I know, but there's something about this dog," I said. "He'll never be a star, he might be an understudy, and anyway, who are you going to adopt him to?" Chico had looked into my eyes and instantly connected somewhere deep inside. It's as if he said, "If you save me, I'll save you back." By now I had had enough experience to go with that feeling.

My next stop was a Petco in northern New Jersey to see Taco. He and his sister Bell were in a pet shop where they hadn't been sold, and the owner decided to euthanize them rather than discount them. The local vet persuaded the owner to relinquish them to rescue. Taco was very shy and quiet from being raised in a cage. This sort of situation is very sad. It reminds me of the psychological experiments they used to do on monkeys, where they would deprive them of socialization to see how it affected their development. Taco was seeing the world for the first time as an adult. Everything was new, and Taco had very slowly started to acclimate. In these cases you can only go as far as the dog wishes. I sat next to him, and after a while, I held him. He was apprehensive—not terrified, but concerned. He didn't bite to get away, but he wanted to go back to what was familiar. I said I thought I could rehabilitate him. The rescue people listened intently and said they would consider it and get back to me.

Dorothy, Jenna, and I went back later that week to adopt Chico. When he saw me, I felt there was a twinge of recognition. I took him out, walked him, and explained to Jenna how you can't approach this dog like another dog. Everything was going great. I signed the adoption papers, but as we were leaving, I went to adjust the neckpiece on his harness and he whipped around and bit my finger. It was my own fault. I joked that we had found one of his triggers, but that's when it sunk in. *What had I gotten myself into?*

We got home and training started immediately. Chico had to learn that people are friends. First, basic training would teach him there were rewards for listening to us. Second, he had to learn biting was not the answer when he didn't get what he wanted. We kept a leash on him at all times, so if he got aggressive, we could control him without getting next to his body. When he growled or snapped, we invented a command called *No mouth* to identify what he was doing wrong. The first few days were very rough, but what was unusual was he knew our family had no malice toward him, and he immediately took to us. He didn't listen to us, but he would include us in his world.

Within a week, the producers called saying they had to film a promo for the San Francisco tryout at a hotel in New York City. They wanted a blonde Chihuahua to do a trick with the director. I hadn't told the producers about Chico because I had so many reservations. I told them I didn't have a trained Chihuahua available, but that I had just adopted one.

"Bring him!" they said.

I tried to explain that he was slightly difficult and that we were assessing him. If I told the truth, then there would have been a prejudice against him, so I warned if he became unsettled, I would just take him away, and we wouldn't have a Chihuahua for the shoot. They were willing to take that chance. Dorothy came to the shoot with me because she knew all the producers, and I needed backup. The door opened and the producing, creative, and marketing staff all screamed in delight. Chico went into full attack mode in my arms. I held him and covered his face until he calmed down. We went in, and I took turns greeting everyone as I explained to them that Chico was overstimulated and needed to get acclimated. I put him down on his leash and he started sniffing the room, barking at everyone in his way.

Jerry Mitchell, who had been in the other room preparing, came in, yelling, "Where's Bruiser? I hear a dog here!" I tried to calm Chico, who erupted in barking. Jerry said, "Dogs love me. Just let him go." I asked Jerry to get down because he is so tall, and he lay down on the bed. Chico dragged me over to the bed, jumped up on Jerry, and licked his face. Jerry was laughing, and Chico was having a great time. Everyone else in the room, including me, was incredulous. There are people who love dogs and there are people who *understand* dogs. Jerry understood dogs, and Chico decided in that moment, Jerry could join our club. I had a second of optimism watching them bond, but this was still miles away from being onstage.

An hour later we were in the other room. For the spot, Chico had to go to Jerry with a note attached to his collar. I gave Jerry a treat and we rolled the camera for the first take. Chico ran to Jerry, got the treat, and Jerry took the note off his collar. As Jerry read the note, Chico gave him a look. On the second take, Chico growled as Jerry went toward his neck. I expressed my concern about a third take, but we rolled anyway. Chico growled again, but I was impressed because he didn't bite. In one week maybe we had taught him to think before biting. We went into the other room to wait. Jerry came in again and Chico ran over to him, acting like a little puppy. He wouldn't let Jerry pick him up, but he loved being petted by him. Jerry said, "I love this dog. He's going to be great." I didn't have the heart to tell him Chico was still on my "maybe" list.

As for the bulldog, we contacted Karen Massaro, head of the Connecticut branch of the Bulldog Club of America Rescue Network. Karen was a breeder who opened her home to displaced bulldogs. We had used her bulldogs for commercials over the years, and she knew and trusted us. At the time we called, she was holding a bunch of dogs that had been seized from a cruelty case. A farm in northwestern Connecticut had been raided, and in one of the barns were five bulldogs in crates that were being used for breeding. The dogs were in bad shape, and the state police had called Karen to hold them as evidence. One dog was so bad, he had to be euthanized. She kept two of the dogs,

The faces of *Legally Blonde*—Chico with Laura Bell Bundy as Elle Woods. *Photo by Paul Kolnik, courtesy of the Broadway production of* Legally Blonde The Musical

and her staff took the other two. The smallest was a three-year-old female named Zizi.

Like Taco, Zizi was sweet with people but had no idea what the world was. Karen thought she'd be perfect for us, so we became her foster home. Zizi took a while to get used to the furniture, but the biggest thing she had to get used to was freedom. At our house she could run and jump and sleep anywhere she wanted. It was a joy to watch her blossom.

In April of that year we were approved to adopt Taco, who we renamed Teddy. By then we'd had Chico a month, and his behavior was improving, but it was hard to tell if he would be ready by opening night in San Francisco.

Elle Woods was being played by Laura Bell Bundy. The first day of rehearsals for the workshop, she came to us with gifts for Chico—a bowl, a leash, and a collar—which we immediately put on him. It was a gesture that was only the beginning of a great relationship, and Laura was immediately added to Chico's club. Chico, of course, went crazy when he saw Jerry Mitchell. As promised, we didn't demand rehearsal with the actors. The dogs were happy being there, and just meeting the people and getting used to the routine was enough.

We explained Chico's past to the company and asked that they give him space and let him approach on his own time. Chico had learned some basic commands, and in two days of running the opening scene, he was actually doing exactly what was in the script. This dog, that could be petted by only three other people besides Dorothy and me, had learned at a rate that I had never seen before. And three weeks later, he performed flawlessly in front of a room filled with fifty backers. The workshop proved so successful they went full steam ahead with the out-of-town tryout. We would rehearse in New York City, and then go to San Francisco with performances in January and February. There would be a two-week break, two weeks of rehearsal in New York, and then we'd open at the Palace Theater in April.

A photo session was set up for Laura and Chico that became the poster art for the show. In my whole career, a dog's role was never recognized to the point that it symbolized the show. It was quite an honor. I felt confident that if he could control his aggression, Chico was our guy.

Because it was a long prep time and a long out-of-town tryout, Dorothy decided to leave her administrative job and work with me. We would turn it into a family adventure. We would pull Jenna, now nine, out of school for six months, tutor her in San Francisco, and then enroll her in New York in the spring. With the two Chihuahuas, bulldog, and understudies, we'd need two handlers. Housing and transportation were almost as expensive as they had been on *Chitty Chitty Bang Bang*, and they had not budgeted money for this. The only way to reduce our costs was to use one Chihuahua onstage instead of two and make it a one-trainer show. We'd have to compensate the single trainer for all the extra work with the bulldogs, but we could cut costs on salaries, housing, and travel. My only request was that the managers tell the creators that their artistic vision was being reduced for financial reasons as opposed to our inability to deliver the performances.

While this was going on, I got a call from Mike Nichols. We had stayed in touch and worked together a few times since he had produced *Annie*. He was getting ready to begin shooting a movie called *Charlie Wilson's War*, staring Tom Hanks and Julia Roberts. A month before shooting, he decided Julia's character needed dogs and Tom's character needed cats. At a production meeting he mentioned this detail and finished by saying, "And get this guy Bill Berloni in New York. I've worked with him, and he's great." The Hollywood people couldn't understand why, with all the great trainers in LA, he wanted me. The hierarchy in Hollywood is very different than Broadway—animal trainers rank somewhere well below the caterers in importance. But it was an opportunity I couldn't pass up. I would do anything to work for Mike.

The shooting for *Charlie Wilson's War* coincided with rehearsals of *Legally Blonde* in New York City, but wrapped the day before the company traveled to San Francisco. Dorothy could set up the rehearsals of *Legally*

A couple of showgirls—Orfeh and Chloe.
Photo by Paul Kolnik, courtesy of the Broadway production of Legally Blonde The Musical

Blonde in New York, then she and Jenna would return to the farm when the show went to San Francisco. Universal Pictures agreed to fly me back and forth to New York, first class, in between shots for *Charlie Wilson's War*. They put me and my trainers up in Beverly Hills for the movie, and the dogs even got their own trailer when we were on location. Thanks to Mike, I was treated like royalty.

We found our second bulldog for *Legally Blonde* through Bulldog Rescue in October. Her name was Chloe. A husband got her in a divorce settlement, and she was living in his garage. He finally decided to give her up. Because she was more outgoing, we decided she would be our performer and Zizi would be the understudy. In the months since August, when the second Chihuahua was cut, we'd been looking for an understudy, since Teddy was too shy to do Chico's role. We looked at dozens of dogs. Two days before I left for Hollywood, I was dropping off a dog at the Connecticut Humane Society. The head trainer asked if I had ever found that Chihuahua I was looking for. She said she had a dog that had come in a month ago that needed medical attention and had just hit the adoption floor. She asked if I would like to see him. I was all packed and ready to go, but out of courtesy, I said, "Sure."

In comes this 5-pound, red Chihuahua/Pomeranian mix named Boo Boo, barking like he's a guard dog. He was a little smaller than Chico, but fuzzy, and he had that attitude. He had no idea that he was the size of a squirrel. I played with him, picked him up, and he licked the inside of my ears. I liked him, but I actually had a pit bull in the car and couldn't take him at that moment. I called Dorothy and asked if she could come the next day to see him. Of course, she and Jenna fell in love with Boo Boo, and he came into our lives one week before the first rehearsal of *Legally Blonde*.

I was able to be there for the first five days of rehearsal. There had been a few cast changes—Margo, the character who played with Bruiser in the first scene, was now played by Annaleigh Ashford, a talented, loving young woman whom Chico took to right away. The hairdresser who owns the bulldog was now being played by a multitalented actress named Orfeh, who also understood animals. Her husband Andy was playing the UPS driver. Chloe instantly fell in love with both of them. The script had been cut to accommodate the one Chihuahua, but the opening cue was perfect, so it hadn't changed.

I had hired Kirsten from *Inishmore* to assist Dorothy, and everyone saw how well two trainers worked. Two weeks before we were to leave New York to go to San Francisco, management changed their minds—they said they would pay for the second trainer. It was a little daunting, but we were able to arrange Jenna's schooling and find a house and pet sitter at the last minute.

Thirteen days later Dorothy and Jenna flew to San Francisco with Chico and Boo Boo under their seats. Because we never fly our animals in the holds of planes, we arranged for Chloe to be driven out to San Francisco. I wrapped the film and drove to San Francisco to meet up with everyone. We spent our first Sunday morning together as a family in over two months in our San Francisco apartment. I was drinking coffee, Jenna was watching TV, Dorothy was reading the paper. Chico and Boo Boo were wrestling on the hardwood floor as they had been for the last seven weeks. Right in front of our eyes, Chico flipped Boo over and he landed with a thud. He lay there motionless, his body limp. He wasn't breathing and his eyes were rolling back in his head. By now I had held enough dogs in their final moments to

"I'm having a very bad day." Chico at the Associated Humane Society.

know when they're slipping away. Not wanting Jenna to see him die, I said, "He's okay. I'm going to take him into the bedroom." I turned to Dorothy and said, "Call a vet."

As I lay his limp body on the bed, I knelt down, telling him to stay with us. I checked his lips and they were turning blue. Dorothy said, "Is he alive?" I turned to her and said, "No. We've lost him." I heard her shriek in anguish. I heard Jenna start to cry. Something in my mind refused to let this happen. I picked up his little head, cupped his mouth, and began doing doggy CPR that I had only read about once. Just then, whomever Dorothy was calling picked up the phone, and through her tears, she explained that we were visiting San Francisco and our dog had just died. Just then, after five breaths, Boo Boo coughed. "Wait—he took a breath" I said.

The vet's office was a half-mile down the road. The staff was great. By the time the doctor actually came in, Boo was starting to stand. The doctor did a quick exam as I was explaining his history. The doctor was amazed. Outside of an irregular heartbeat, Boo seemed to be okay. They would keep him for a while, giving him steroids to reduce the brain swelling and just to make sure his heart stabilized, but if all that checked out, he would be fine. The doctor said, "Good work on your part. You saved his life." We went to bed exhausted that night to get ready to start our first day of technical rehearsals.

The last real phase of training was acclimating Chico to the set, stage, and audience. I kept hoping the courage he showed me in Newark, attacking tractor-trailers, would carry over. In New York, an hour had been set aside for us to rehearse everyone who handled the animals. While we expected the same here, the stagehand union rules prohibited it. We could walk onstage for five minutes every one and a half hours. The first day we didn't get to Chico's first cue. I understood everyone was scrambling to get the sets up, so we were patient. The second day, there still was no time for us, but we did get to the cue. I carried Chico out to center stage. When he saw Annaleigh Ashford, the actress who worked with him in the first scene, he barked fine but was very nervous in the big space. By the end of that third day, there was still no rehearsal for Chico. I made my concerns known. Management said there was no time to rehearse, plus no money to pay overtime to have the crew work through dinner.

Then the second miracle of the week happened. Our crew head from New York had refrained from asking the local crew for any favors because they were working so hard. But on the third day, he mentioned it, and to his surprise they said, "We know Bill. We like him and his dogs. Let him do whatever he wants." Over the years I had been in San Francisco many times. We treat everyone we work with, including the crew, with respect. The crew has talents that the audience doesn't see, but they are no less important than anyone else. That one act of kindness to me made the show happen for the dogs. Each dinner and supper break, Dorothy and I would sit with Chico onstage. It took him about a week to feel comfortable in the space.

Chloe, our second bulldog, had been caught in a Colorado snowstorm for three days on her trip west. No worse for wear, she was ready to go. When she saw Orfeh and her husband Andy, she went crazy. She, too, needed a week to get used to the space.

Soon, our first preview arrived. Chico sensed everyone was nervous backstage, and he was a little distracted. The first audience was so excited to see the world premiere of this musical. The overture started and the audience screamed. The curtain went up, and the audience screamed. The first set change happened, and the audience screamed. Then Chico hit the stage, and they roared. His ears were pinned back as he went to Annaleigh. He barked because he loved her, but he couldn't wait to get into her arms and offstage. He was nervous for the rest of the show, but Laura and Annaleigh protected him. At the curtain call, I told Laura to come and get him instead of sending him out into that thunderous applause. Jerry Mitchell saw how the audience affected Chico. Jerry made sure before each rehearsal that week that we got his set, Annaleigh, and the girls so we could run his scene and reassure him he was safe. With those rehearsals and a lot of love, it took Chico a week or so to completely ignore the audience and get into his show.

The following weeks there, we worked long and hard. We rehearsed every day with the cast and crew. We did interviews. The company slept, ate, and breathed that show. Changes were constantly being made, and new songs were going in and out. But it all came together. Reviews were positive. By the time we left San Francisco, the only thing left was to teach Chloe to bow.

When I drove up to the Palace Theater, there was a 50-foot-high billboard of Laura and Chico. His face became part of the logo—on the marquee, in the merchandising, in ads, taxicabs, commercials—anywhere you can imagine, there was Chico. Chloe had been so well accepted in San Francisco that they decided to add a second scene for her in the second act. She was so excited to be working with the two people she loved the most that on the second night, she threw up, which is what bulldogs do when they're excited. I took it as a sign of love and affection. It got a huge laugh.

Opening night came. We loaded into a stretch limo to go to the opening-night party. I kissed Dorothy and Jenna as they got out with Chloe, who was wearing a pink sequined dress that Dorothy had made, to walk the red carpet. The door closed. The cue came for me to come out. I was in my tux, Chico in a sequined tux. Before I opened the door, I closed my eyes and saw all the animals I had owned, gathered together with Sandy in the middle, smiling, giving us their blessing.

As Chico and I stood on the red carpet, it was a special moment. It is what every entertainer dreams about. But I'm also an animal trainer. There are still a lot of animals to rescue and lots of opening nights to come.

Chapter 22

Thinking about Tomorrow

It looked like 2008 was going to be a great year. *Legally Blonde* was a hit. With its positive messages about empowerment and being true to yourself, and the enormous energy of the cast, it had become one of my favorite shows. Our audiences loved it. So it looked like we would be settling in for a long run, but two things happened to slow us down. First, although we were nominated for seven Tony Awards, we didn't win any. That hurt the marketing for the show. We were still getting enthusiastic audiences, but we weren't selling out anymore. Then the recession hit Broadway, and ticket sales really fell. *Legally Blonde* closed in October of that year.

I started looking for new opportunities. During a recession, producers tend to do more revivals because the costs can be lower, and it's easier to attract audiences to shows that are familiar. That didn't worry me because there were three major revivals in the works that all featured animals, at least as originally written and performed. So I thought there would be lots of work.

First there was *Gypsy*. I had just done the Broadway revival starring Bernadette Peters a couple of years before, and I knew many people in the cast and crew. The fact that Gypsy Rose Lee and her sister June Havoc had pets all their lives was written into the musical for a reason, but the producers decided to use puppets instead of real animals.

"Hey, Mister, which way to 42nd street and Broadway?" *Photo copyright © 2012 by Rachael L. Ledbetter, Dapper Dogs, Inc.*

The second show was *Miracle Worker*, the first Broadway revival since the original production many years before. I had done the play in regional theater a number of times over the years, and I had worked with the producer, Randall Wreghitt, on *The Lieutenant of Inishmore*. There is a pivotal scene where the audience realizes that Helen Keller is making progress when she tries to talk to her dog using sign language, but as costs increased, producers cut the dog.

Two down, one to go, and I thought this was a sure thing. The Roundabout Theatre Company was doing a revival of the 1987 Lincoln Center production of *Anything Goes*. I had supplied the dogs for that show, and I had worked with the director, Kathleen Marshall, on *Two Gentlemen of Verona*. Cole Porter, Guy Bolton, and P. G. Wodehouse must have felt that the aristocracy and their pampered pooches were significant enough to write them into the show, but the Roundabout was in the same financial crunch as everyone else. No dog.

I understood that everyone on Broadway was hurting, but I still question the choice of cutting the animals. Why must the animals be the first to go? The savings weren't great. An animal's weekly cost is less than the weekly salary of one actor.

My ultimate concern is for the people seeing those revivals for the first time. They might think that real animals were never used in those shows. In each of these plays, the animals were important to the plot—that's why the writers put them in. To me, that's not a revival, but a re-write, and it should be credited that way so the audience knows.

Don't get me wrong, Broadway has provided me with a career and the opportunity to work with some of the most brilliant and talented people in the world. But it was clear that the New York theater in 2009 was not interested in trained animals, at least not until the recession ended. So to pay the bills I hit the road. We had two years of a successful Equity tour of *Legally Blonde* and then a year of a non-Equity tour. For the tours we trained a new Bruiser, a little Chihuahua named Frankie rescued from the Meriden Humane Society in Meriden, Connecticut. He was a stray that the rescue group brought to my vet. When my vet heard Frankie was up for adoption, he recommended me, and a star was born. His understudy, Roxie, was saved by a woman named Rocky

Gates who runs CHIPPS (Chihuahua and Pounds Pups Rescue) in Louisiana. Roxie was a tough little survivor. She was so confident and unafraid of the world she must have been a stray for a long time. To play Rufus the bulldog, we rescued China and Nellie. China also came from Rocky Gates. She had been turned in because she was too much to handle. Her understudy, Nellie, was a puppy surrendered to the Humane Society of New York because she was out of control. With a job and a purpose they calmed right down.

Of course, there were lots of productions of *Annie* and *The Wizard of Oz*. We also did regional theater, summer stock, community theater, and even school plays, which we do just because we love it. In fact, a production of *Annie* at my daughter's school gave us all a chance to work together. Jenna played one of the orphans, Dorothy came out of "acting retirement" to play Miss Hannigan, and I provided the dog.

We also started dreaming of something big all our own. Dorothy had managed to get the stage rights to *Because of Winn-Dixie*, the wonderful children's book by Kate DiCamillo that had been made into a movie starring AnnaSophie Robb and Jeff Daniels. Then, in 2009, she found two deerhound/borzoi puppies, Izzy and Phoebe, who looked exactly like the illustration on the front of the book. When she asked me if we could adopt them, I thought she was crazy. We had no script, no songs, and we were years away from production. Why would we get the dogs?

"Research," she answered. She wanted to see if we could train these huge dogs for the stage. I figured that the fact that these dogs had become available at the same time and resembled each other so closely was a kind of omen, so we adopted Izzy from St. Louis and Phoebe from San Diego.

Deerhounds and borzois are sight hounds, like greyhounds. They are difficult to train for obedience because they are easily stimulated—every little sight or sound distracts them. After a year of training, I was ready to give up, when we were asked to provide dogs for a Manhattan Theater Club revival of Edna Ferber's *The Royal Family*. Izzy and Phoebe had the right look and the part was easy. All they had to do was walk on with the leading man, stand center stage, then exit.

"Can you believe
we're not related?"
Photo © Mary Bloom

I had one of my longtime handlers, Brian Hoffman, work with me on running the show. Unfortunately, Izzy and Phoebe weren't in love with the stage. The dogs loved the quiet apartment, Central Park at night, and the dressing room. Everywhere else, they were anxious and concerned. We got them through the eight-week run and then retired them to our farm. We'd have to look elsewhere for a dog to play Winn-Dixie.

Around that time, our longtime friend and New York general manager Wendy Orshan called saying that she was representing a new producer, Arielle Tepper Madover. Arielle had become a successful producer at a very young age and is still much younger than most Broadway producers. She's also a wonderful human being. Arielle and Wendy were working on the thirty-fifth anniversary revival of *Annie*. Wendy set up a meeting, and two days after Arielle accepted the best play Tony Award for *Red*, I was in her office.

Arielle told me that her lifelong love of musical theater had started with seeing the original Broadway production of *Annie*, with my Sandy and the actress Allison Smith, when she was eight years old. She was planning a first-class revival that would be directed by the legendary writer/director James Lapine. It would mark the first time I would be working on a Broadway production of *Annie* without Martin Charnin, the director who gave me my start. The show would open in the fall of 2012. Arielle and Wendy explained that they wanted to create a marketing campaign focused on the search for Sandy instead of the search for Annie.

I thought I was dreaming. On top of everything else, Arielle proposed doing a documentary called *Searching for Sandy* that would cover the entire process, from the shelter through training to the stage. I couldn't believe it. This could create great publicity for Broadway and for animal welfare. My message of animal rescue would be front and center. For shelter dogs, this could mean a much brighter tomorrow.

Of course, that tomorrow was more than two years away. In the meantime, there were more tours, small theatrical productions, and a Disney television movie called *Frenemies* that starred one of our agency dogs, Winston, owned by Theresa Carroll.

Every leading man on Broadway needs two gorgeous girls at his side. *Photo by Joan Marcus*

But the months following the meeting were very tough for me. My father had been fighting Parkinson's disease for more than a decade. In the fall of 2010 he required full-time care, and for the first time I had to take over my parents' affairs. It's a task I took on without question. We enjoyed our last Christmas together in 2010, and in March of 2011 my father passed away.

As an only child, husband, and father myself, I had to take care of everybody over those last months. My father was buried on a Saturday and the next day I had to leave for a production of *Annie* in New Jersey. Fewer than twenty-four hours after my father's burial, I found myself alone in a hotel room at the Jersey Shore. That first Monday at rehearsal was tough. I got through it, but Tuesday morning I woke up very low, lonely and exhausted, missing my dad terribly. What could possibly help?

Just then my cell phone rang. It was Allen Wasser, who had been the general manager of *Chitty Chitty Bang Bang* on Broadway. He said he was honored to tell me that I was going to be the recipient of the 2011 Tony Honor for Excellence in Theater. For a moment, I didn't believe him. I never expected to win a Tony Honor. For one thing, I wasn't eligible. You must belong to one of the theater unions to be eligible to win a Tony Award and there's no union for animal trainers. But the Tony committee has special categories for people like me who play major roles but are ineligible in all the other categories.

I remember babbling my thanks. My hands were shaking as I called my wife, who cried, and then my mother. Next I felt moved to call Martin Charnin, the original director of *Annie,* and Michael Price, the original producer, and pass on the good news and thank them for believing in this young kid and giving him a chance. Moments before I had been in the depths of despair, but the one impossible dream for a theater person had come true. I accepted the award in May 2011.

In December 2011, I got the green light to begin our search for the next Sandy. James Lapine wanted dogs that hadn't appeared on stage before, and Arielle wanted to publicize our efforts to find them. Dorothy began the search on Petfinder.com, but we ran into an unexpected snag. Generally, we adopt our dogs in Connecticut, New York, or New Jersey. This time, there were very few medium-sized "Sandy" dogs available for adoption in the tri-state area. I wondered if thirty years of *Annie* on stage had changed the fate of these mixed-breed mutts and made them popular pets. I didn't have any hard data, but I know for one of just a few times we had to expand our search across the country.

As we started showing dogs to James, Arielle, and Wendy, most didn't make it past the review. "This one is too big." "This one is too small." "This one is cute but not cute enough." Thanks to the show, dogs that we found in kill shelters and that had no other chances left *were* getting a second chance. I had arranged for the Humane Society of New York to take the dogs that didn't make it through the search until we could find them homes. So even the dogs who lost the part would win a wonderful new life.

We ended up with four dogs to see in person: one in Indiana and three in Tennessee and Alabama. The first dog I saw was named Bart Starr. He looked just like the original comic strip Sandy, with pointy ears, a curly red coat, and a big smile. He was a feral dog from the Bahamas who was sent to a rescue group in Indiana called Homeward Bound. The group treated him for parasites and heartworm, and when he was healthy he was put up for adoption. They said he was two years old and very friendly.

"A rescue dog and a Tony Honor. It doesn't get any better than this."
Photo by Anita and Steve Shevett

When I finally met Bart, he was a great dog. Even though he looked nothing like my other Sandys, I said I wanted to take him to New York to audition. When I did, people at the shelter began to cry. Strangely enough, I cried, too. Why was I so moved? I've rescued hundreds of dogs, but saying

yes to Bart caught me by surprise. What would my original Sandy think? Would he approve? I somehow felt his presence on that day and knew I was on the right path and everything would be alright with Bart.

The other three dogs were all in kill shelters. After meeting them I decided two of them, Sydney and Billy, were too shy to be performers. I need dogs that come charging out of the gate to meet people. Sometimes, I can work with a shy dog if we have enough time, but *Annie* was on a very tight schedule. Rehearsal time was limited, and there was no pre-Broadway tour to learn the part and get used to the crowds. We arranged for the shelters to keep Sydney and Billy until they could be adopted. If there were any issues, they promised I could take the dogs to the Humane Society of New York for adoption there.

Porky was a very different story.

Porky was a stray when she came into the shelter in Columbia, Tennessee. The shelter had no luck placing her. In this rural area, people tend to have either working dogs or hunting dogs. As a large terrier who needed a lot of training, attention, and exercise, Porky was the wrong dog in the wrong place.

Porky did actually make it out of the shelter for a while. A local high school boy brought her home as part of a program in which students take care of dogs and try to find them homes. When the program was over, the boy had wanted to adopt Porky, but the family already had a dog. Even though the two animals had gotten along well, the boy's parents didn't want a second dog.

So Porky went back to the shelter, and her time ran out.

She was led into the euthanasia room and placed on the table. The vet tech prepared the injection and was about to administer the shot. At the last second, Porky slipped free of her collar and jumped into the arms of a prison inmate, a trustee who had been in charge of her care at the shelter. He begged them to spare her life. Everyone was so moved that they agreed to give her forty-eight more hours.

And that's where we came into the story. The shelter didn't put a listing for Porky on Petfinder.com. Instead, Sonya Dickson Rine, the president of the local rescue group, Pet Pals, sent out an emergency message to an animal rescue e-mail list. The first part of the message was written from Porky's point of view and included a picture of her poking her head out of the window of a big, black car. It said:

> *Save This Leading Lady—Tomorrow May Be Too Late!*
> *. . . Hi, obviously my name is Sandy, and I should be in the starring role in* Annie, *but I made one wrong turn and find myself in jail (Maury County Animal Shelter) . . . I don't belong in jail. And worse, they call me Porky. Seriously, I'm not a pig. I'm a Sandy! A beautiful dog star of stage and screen, or even better—your home!*

Following this was an entreaty by the staff members at the shelter:

> *Please help Sandy (aka Porky). She has been at the shelter too long. She was to be euthanized but got loose and ran to one of the trustees working at the shelter. She jumped into his arms, and the shelter employees just couldn't put her to sleep. They have given her more time . . . but just a little. She is spayed and UTD on shots.*

She needs a rescue and one that knows terriers. She is a beautiful Airedale mix [who is] full of herself and life. She needs a brisk walk and lots of play time everyday. Life in a cage is not good for this star. Tomorrow, tomorrow, please change her name and address tomorrow. Save Sandy (aka Porky).

The message was forwarded to my wife. Dorothy forwarded it to me. I sent it to Wendy and Arielle. Their reaction was immediate. Wendy replied: "Her story, her face. This one is so special. It's like she lived just for us."

Arielle agreed. We would rescue Porky, even if she wasn't right for the show.

When I contacted Sonya, at first she thought it was a prank. She and the shelter workers had no idea that a revival of *Annie* was in the works and that we were conducting a search. When I convinced them that I really was who I said I was and that I wanted to see Porky, they immediately put her in a foster home until I could get to Tennessee.

When I arrived, the shelter workers and volunteers treated me a like a hero. Then they brought out Porky, and I knew we had made the right decision. She was happy and friendly, impressing me with her personality. Again I thought about my original Sandy, who was also just hours away from being put down when I found him. I knew, like him, Porky had beaten the odds and could be a winner. When I said I wanted to bring her to New York as a candidate, there were smiles and tears all around. It became a big story and was even covered on the local news.

By February 2012, we had two good candidates, Bart and Porky, for James and Arielle. During the process, one of the show's sponsors asked if we could look in its targeted markets. Two weeks after we ended the search, we decided to give it one more try. Dorothy spent the weekend doing another search in those cities and found one more dog. She had eyes that reminded me of my original Sandy, she was in a kill shelter in Houston called BARC, and she had less than twenty-four hours to live. She was a stray that was in pretty good condition but she had lacerations on her back left leg that needed medical attention. I instantly called the shelter, spoke to a manager, and put a twenty-four-hour hold on the dog. After consulting Arielle, I had a former handler in Houston, Jennifer James, rescue her on my behalf. The shelter immediately had her spayed and her leg treated for us. She had been listed as "Bruno," but we changed her name to Sunny. In my head I felt the sun would come out for her, whether she ever performed or not.

Jennifer starting telling me how great she was. I recommended Sunny as a candidate. Arielle and Wendy wanted her in New York for the audition the following week, but there was a two-week quarantine for ground transport. When I told Arielle, she said, "Do whatever it takes to get her here."

I contacted Rob Cox, another one of my former handlers in Tucson. He flew to Houston, rented a car, picked up Sunny, and drove three days to New York, where she was triaged at the Humane Society of New York and given a clean bill of health. We now had three good candidates for the role of Sandy. Besides my three fully trained Sandy dogs at home, I now had three young, untrained dogs that immediately bonded with each other. Watching them run free and safe from harm in my backyard gave me a lot of joy.

On March 11, 2012, there was a final audition for Sandy. Bart Starr, Porky (now named Casey), and Sunny were ready. We drove the dogs to New York City and met with James and Arielle and the whole *Annie* production team. Everyone had been following the dogs' stories and looked in awe at these three beautiful creatures. After falling in love with all three, James had to make a hard choice.

James felt that audiences might not accept Bart Starr because he didn't look like the stage version of Sandy. It's funny for me to think that we worried that my original Sandy didn't look enough like the cartoon dog, and now Harold Gray's Sandy isn't as recognizable as the image of the dog I found and trained thirty-five years ago. That left Sunny and Casey.

As the room waited for the final call, James eventually said, "I can't decide. Train them both and come back in a month."

It looked like I had to prepare for one last Sandy callback. Bart Starr was adopted by a dear friend of ours. I continued basic training with Casey and Sunny. Both of them were on track and doing very well when I noticed something a little off about Casey's movement. First, when I was teaching her "sit,"

"Bill, where have you been all my life?" Photo © Mary Bloom

she would sit on one hip instead of square on her hind legs. Second, there was a clicking sound in her hips as she sat. And finally, she hopped when she ran. Only someone working with her very closely would notice such subtleties. I took Casey to two vets, did two sets of X-rays, and had our home vet and his orthopedic teams look at the findings. The diagnosis was that Casey had mild hip dysplasia in her left hip and a luxating patella in her right leg. I felt myself getting very emotional. How could this young dog be so damaged? My vet explained that it was hereditary, but there was good news. Her hips could be treated with supplements and therapy, and with surgery we could repair her knee and she could be the understudy. Not only had we saved Casey's life, but we could also provide her with a pain-free existence. I informed Arielle and James, and they gave their blessing to Sunny becoming our new Sandy.

As of this writing, Sunny is in the last stages of training for Sandy. Casey is in physical therapy and soon will be back in training as the understudy. After a nationwide search, the production found its new Annie, a talented young actress by the name of Lilla Crawford, and in August we'll begin rehearsals for the show. I know she and Sunny will go down in theater history as a great team. Sunny and Casey—and Bart Starr, Sydney, and Billy—have entered a long list of dogs, cats, and other animals whose lives were saved through the wonder of Broadway.

In the last five years, Dorothy and I bought a new piece of property in Connecticut. We are keeping it as open space. We've built a new home and barn for us and all of our animals—nearly forty in all. I call it The Home that Sandy Built. It is part of a sanctuary we call Little Arfin' Acres that is not only for the wild animals that inhabit our woods, but also for the pets that nobody wanted and that needed a home. For all of them, and for us, tomorrow has come at last.

Afterword

Everything I know about training animals I learned from my parents.

Before I went off to kindergarten, my parents taught me that all living things—people, dogs, cats, even the plants my dad cared for in his greenhouses—deserve respect and kindness. It was a shock for me when I went to school and first met bullying and meanness. My friends have always been people, like my wonderful wife, Dorothy, who were raised the same way.

So when I first faced the challenge of training an animal for the stage, I didn't do what other dog trainers had been doing. It seemed obvious to me that trying to bully Sandy to do what I wanted him to do wouldn't work. So I did what felt right. I tried to make him feel safe and at home. I encouraged him every time he did something I asked him to do. I moved at his pace. I rewarded him for the right behaviors, but I didn't punish him when he did something wrong—I ignored the wrong behavior and led him to the right one.

I didn't know that this was the beginning of a positive reinforcement method that was ahead of its time and the technique that would define my career. I just thought I was doing what my parents had taught me to do.

Over the past thirty years, this technique has improved based on what I've been taught by every animal I've had the pleasure to share my life with, particularly by what I call my "superdogs"—a

"Don't be afraid to dream big!"
Photo © Mary Bloom